St Paul's
and the City

Frank Atkinson

MICHAEL JOSEPH

PARK LANE PRESS

Acknowledgments

BBC Hulton Picture Library: 65; Bridgeman Art Library Ltd: 28–9, 33, 56, 57 (above), 86; Fine Art Photographs: 6; Guildhall Library, City of London: 10 (above), 16, 19, 26–7, 30–1, 38–9, 72, 72–3, 80; Haslemere Estates: 87 (above); Angelo Hornak: 5, 9, 12–13, 14 (left and right), 15, 17 (left and below), 18, 21, 23, 24 (left and right), 25, 27, 30, 32, 34, 35, 36, 36–7 (above and below), 40, 43, 44, 45, 46, 47, 48, 49, 50, 54, 57 (below left, below centre and below right), 58, 60, 61, 63, 67, 69, 76, 78 (above), 81 (above and below), 82, 83, 87 (below), 89, 90; Jeremy Marks: 78 (below); The Museum of London: 84–5; St Paul's Cathedral: 10–11, 13 (below), 38 (below), 39 (below), 53, 59, 68, 71; The Photo Source Ltd: 74–5; The Press Association Ltd: 20; Don Price: 22, 41.

The publishers gratefully acknowledge permission to reproduce extracts from the following works:

Inge, Dr W.R., *Diary of a Dean* (Hutchinson Publishing Group Limited)

Matthews, Dean W.R., *A History of St Paul's Cathedral* (John Baker)

Matthews, Dean W.R., *Memories and Meanings* © 1969 by W.R. Matthews (Reprinted by permission of Hodder and Stoughton Limited).

This edition published in 1985 by Park Lane Press, 40 Park Street, London W1Y 4DE, who designed and produced the book.

Text copyright © Frank Atkinson 1985

ISBN 0-7181-2629-7

Text set by Servis Filmsetting Ltd, Manchester
Colour origination by Mullis Morgan Ltd, London
Printed and bound by Printer Industria Grafica SA, Barcelona, Spain
D.L.B. 11084-1985

Designer: Adrian Hodgkins
Indexer: Ann Atkinson
Plans: Eugene Fleury

Contents

Author's note

I am grateful to my colleagues in St Paul's Cathedral who have cheerfully suffered much questioning over the past months and especially to Selene Mills and the Reverend Philip Buckler, the Sacrist, who even answered a couple of questionnaires. Many ex-colleagues in the Guildhall Library have been generously helpful and I thank them all. Those I have most persistently pestered are Irene Pollock, Ralph Hyde, John Fisher, Jeremy Smith and, in the art gallery, Vivien Knight; and to them I offer apologies as well as thanks. My thanks also to Angelo Hornak for climbing and scrambling through the cathedral in search of the best pictures. Through the frenzy of meeting yet another deadline, my wife Ann again kept her head whilst I, as usual, lost mine.

St Paul's Cathedral   F.A.

How to use this book

The text has been printed in two colours throughout for easy reference. The black text is a walk-round guide to the cathedral and the magenta text describes related places, institutions and people in the City.

Cathedral opening times

The cathedral is open to visitors daily from 0730 to 1800 hours in summer and 1700 hours in winter. Guided 'Supertours' are conducted from the Friends' Table near the west door at 1100 and 1400 hours every weekday.

The Whispering Gallery, the Stone Gallery, the Golden Gallery, the crypt and the Treasury are open 1000 (Saturday 1100) to 1515. There is an organ recital most Fridays at 1230.

Divine services

Sundays: 0800, 1030 (C), 1130 (C), 1515 (C).
Monday to Friday: 0730, 0800, 1230 (not Friday), 1700 (C), summer/1600 (C) winter.
Saturday: 0730, 0800, 1000 (C), 1230, 1700 (C), summer/1600 (C) winter.
(C) denotes choral service.

The times given are subject to alteration or cancellation because of special events which are held in the cathedral from time to time. For further information please telephone 01–248 2705.

Introduction

The modified Latin cross form of St Paul's Cathedral can be clearly seen amid the post-1945 commercial buildings.

The first church dedicated to St Paul was built in 604 by Ethelbert, King of Kent, for Mellitus, the first Bishop of London. The Saxon church was destroyed by fire and rebuilt a number of times, the last disaster being in 1087 when William II acceded to the throne of England. In that year the building of the Norman cathedral, now known as Old St Paul's, was begun by Maurice, Bishop of London. It was nearly 200 years before the building and embellishment of the cathedral were finished and it became the principal ornament of the City of London.

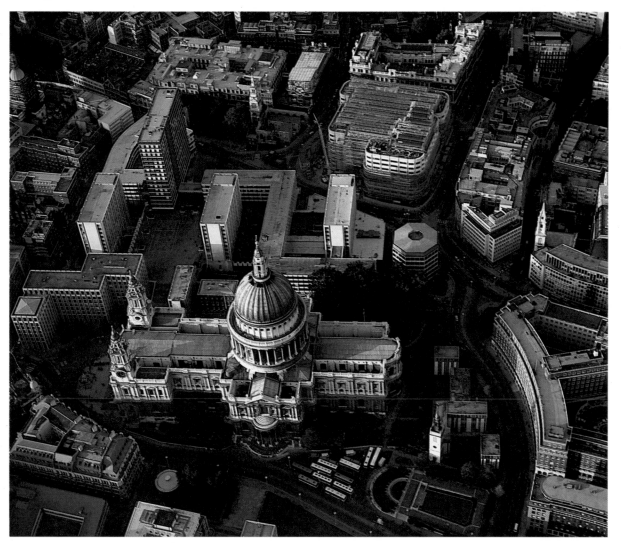

Even before its completion the cathedral was the focal point of everyday life in the City. Paul's Cross was much more than an open-air pulpit for preachers. The cathedral bells summoned the people to Paul's Cross and the surrounding space at the north-east corner of the building for general assemblies called folkmoots; and political debates and even some trials were held there. The idea that St Paul's belonged to the citizens was occasionally taken to excess by some people, leading to mayoral proclamations against misuse of the building. For example, in 1411 the Lord Mayor threatened anyone found wrestling within the Sanctuary with forty days' imprisonment; and in 1554 a mayoral edict forbad the carriage of goods ('beare, bread, fyshe, fruyte and other grosse wares') and the leading of mules, horses and beasts through the cathedral.

The present phase in the close relationship between St Paul's and the City started with yet another rebuilding – this one after the Great Fire of 1666 had destroyed the cathedral and most of the other buildings within the City walls. The man chosen in 1669 to design and construct the new St Paul's, Christopher Wren, was a remarkable polymath – a first-rate Latinist, scientist, anatomist, astronomer, mathematician, engineer and architect. Son of a dean and nephew of a bishop, he was a deeply religious and humane person. Sir Christopher – he was knighted in 1672 – lies buried in the crypt of this cathedral which is generally acknowledged to be not only his masterpiece but also his monument.

The present building was financed by a tax on coal coming into London and by donations from all over England. The City Chamberlain received all the moneys and acted as treasurer for the project. Wren and members of the team of craftsmen he assembled at St Paul's – masons, carvers, smiths and carpenters – were also involved in the building of some fifty churches in the City and a number of secular structures, from Temple Bar in the west to the Monument in the east.

Today the Lord Mayor is still, ex officio, one of the Trustees of St Paul's and has a special stall in the choir. The parade of the Lord Mayor's Show stops at the south portico while the Lord Mayor goes to be greeted by the Dean and Chapter and, during the year of office, he (or she) will attend many cathedral services.

For centuries the City's common seal has had on its obverse side a figure of St Paul, and the arms of the City have included the sword of St Paul, the City's patron saint. There are many other connections between the cathedral and the City dealt with later in the book. What should be mentioned here, however, is the continuing generosity towards St Paul's by the Corporation, the livery companies and a whole range of commercial and financial institutions.

Perhaps members of this last group may feel they receive some small return from the fact that their advertisers commonly use the image of the dome of St Paul's with its ball and cross, flanked by the twin towers, not only as a symbol of the City of London but also as an indication of its probity and reliability.

The West Front

The most familiar face of the cathedral is the WEST FRONT with its steps, portico and three doors, and the dome framed between the two towers. People usually enter by the doors to the north and south of this end but, on special ceremonial occasions, the big middle door is opened for the use of distinguished visitors.

The doors are approached by a double flight of granite steps leading to a marble terrace. The first flight is returned, providing north and south access, while the upper flight is stopped by dwarf walls. The wrought-iron standard lamps on these walls were designed by Edwin Lutyens and were erected in memory of the artist Lord Leighton who is buried in the cathedral. The first flight of steps was relaid in 1873 by the then Surveyor to the Fabric of St Paul's, F. C. Penrose, from the original Wren drawings discovered in the cathedral library.

The west portico is a double portico, the lower part consisting of twelve Corinthian columns, 12 metres (40 feet) high, coupled to form five bays. The upper storey is of eight Composite columns which are 9.9 metres (32 feet 6 inches) high. The middle door, known as the Great West Door, is 8.2 metres (27 feet) high and 3.6 metres (12 feet) wide.

In the triangular pediment of the portico is a bas-relief sculpture by Francis Bird depicting the conversion of St Paul. Over the great door there is another bas-relief of St Paul preaching to the people of Berea. This, and the six smaller sculpted scenes from St Paul's life at the same level – three to the north and three to the south – are all by Francis Bird, as are the seven rooftop statues. Christopher Wren gave Bird a great deal of work to do both outside and inside the cathedral, as will be seen throughout this book.

The records of the City of London contain an order dated 3 May 1633 of the Star Chamber court regarding 'some differences lately arisen between the Lord Mayor and the Dean and Chapter of St Paul's concerning the carrying up of the Lord Mayor's sword within the Cathedral and especially within the Choir. . . .' Counsel for both sides were directed to meet to settle the matter.

More than 300 years later Dean Matthews in his autobiography *Memories and Meanings* (1969) dealt with what he called 'a friendly controversy with the Corporation'. This was the question of where the Lord Mayor should greet the monarch when royal personages arrived by car directly at the west front of the cathedral without first being received at Temple Bar. 'We did not wish to concede', he wrote, 'even in ceremonial, that the City Corporation had any authority in St Paul's. . . .' Admitting that there was a humorous, if not childish, side to this, he continued:

It struck me as ludicrous that virgers and other officials should have to keep a sharp watch on the Lord Mayor and aldermen to prevent them from coming too far up the steps with the King and Queen, while we were not looking.

A rehearsal in the Ringing Chamber in the north-west tower.

The three pediment statues are of St Paul, at the apex, with St Peter to the left and St James to the right. The four evangelists are on the towers: Matthew and Mark on the north tower and Luke and John on the south.

The two towers, 73.6 metres (221 feet) high, are particularly interesting in that they accord both with the angular form of the west face and with the circular shape of the dome. The change takes place at colonnade level and finishes with cupolas topped by gilded copper pineapples. These finials were cast by the founder, Jane Brewer, from a model made by Francis Bird.

Samuel Fulkes, who carved the capitals to the west portico, was appointed by Wren to be the mason in charge of the NORTH-WEST TOWER. Inside this tower, at the level of the statues of St Matthew and St Mark, is the belfry. The Book of Common Prayer of 1662 directed that:

> All Priests and Deacons are to say daily the Morning and Evening Prayer . . . and the Curate that ministereth in every Parish Church and Chapel shall say the same . . . where he ministereth, and shall cause a Bell to be tolled thereunto a convenient time before he begin, that the people may come to hear God's Word and to pray with him.

So, in 1700, a single bell was installed in the north-west tower. It is still there and is rung for five minutes before some weekday services and the eight o'clock Sunday morning service. Yet almost 200 years had passed after the completion of the tower before a ring of bells was hung in October 1878. The twelve bells had been cast earlier that year by John Taylor & Sons.

A short service of dedication was held in the ringing chamber after Evensong on All Saints' Day 1878, conducted by the Bishop of London. When the service ended the bells were rung for over an hour. The ringers were all members of the Ancient Society of College Youths, a society of bellringers founded in 1637. Today's St Paul's Cathedral Guild of Ringers are also members of the College Youths.

Some of the special events for which the bells of St Paul's have been rung include Dean Gregory's 80th birthday – 9 February 1899; the end of the First World War – 11 November 1918; the coronation days of King George VI in 1937 and Queen Elizabeth II in 1952; the Silver Jubilee of the reign of HM The Queen in 1977 and, in July 1981, the wedding of the Prince and Princess of Wales.

In November 1875 the Lord Mayor chaired a meeting at the Mansion House to launch an appeal for funds to provide a ring of bells for the cathedral and a Bell Committee was formed. Soon a leaflet, printed in copperplate type, was produced and distributed. It read:

St Paul's is nearly the only Cathedral in England which does not possess a Peal of Bells.

Placed as it is in the Centre of the Metropolis, where it is especially called upon to give expression to the Nation's joys and sorrows, it greatly needs a Peal of Bells to assist it in the Work.

Sir Christopher Wren provided a Tower to hold a large Peal of Bells, but for 200 years this provision has not been utilized.

The Committee earnestly hope that you will help forward this interesting and important Work.

Within a year sufficient money had been subscribed to provide a ring of twelve bells and to pay for the neces-sary construction work in the tower to support them. The bells are inscribed with the names and mottoes of the donors. Four of the lighter ones were presented by Baroness Burdett-Coutts and the Turners' Company and two by the Drapers' Company. Other companies which presented a bell are the Salters', Merchant Taylors', Fish-mongers', Clothworkers' and Gro-cers'. The tenor bell, which weighs almost as much as the six lightest ones together, was the gift of the Corporation.

The Mermaid Theatre at Puddle Dock, near Blackfriars station, was the first theatre to be built in the City of London for 300 years. It was built on the site of a war-damaged warehouse, the lease of which was granted to Bernard Miles (now Lord Miles) and his company by the City Corporation in October 1956.

On 28 May 1959 at six o'clock in the evening the bells of St Paul's were rung to celebrate the opening of the Mermaid for the first performance of its first production.

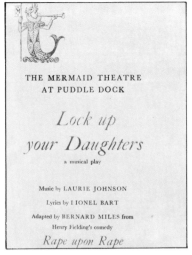

THE MERMAID THEATRE
AT PUDDLE DOCK

Lock up your Daughters

a musical play

Music by LAURIE JOHNSON

Lyrics by LIONEL BART

Adapted by BERNARD MILES from
Henry Fielding's comedy

Rape upon Rape

The mason appointed to the SOUTH-WEST TOWER was John Thompson, who died in 1700; but it is mostly the work of William Kempster who had been in Thompson's employ. Kempster secured the contract some time before Thompson's death.

This tower houses the clock and its three dials facing west, south and east. The dials are 5.1 metres (17 feet) in diameter. The first clock, which was made by Langley Bradley in 1708, had to be replaced in 1719 because of either faulty workmanship or, according to Bradley, tampering with the works by members of the public who were permitted to view the clock. The present instrument was made by John Smith & Sons of Derby and installed in 1893. At the same time the third dial, facing east, was added. The clock is still serviced and maintained by the same firm.

The chimes are struck on two bells known as quarter jacks, which were made in 1707 by Richard Phelps and weigh 640 kg (1409 lb) and 1259 kg (2770 lb) respectively. Phelps also made, in 1716, the hour bell weighing 5294 kg (11,648 lb). This bell, in addition to being struck by a hammer on the hour, also has a clapper which enables it to be tolled. The occasions on which this happens are: the death of a member of the Royal Family, and the death in office of the Archbishop of Canterbury, the Bishop of London, the Dean of St Paul's and the Lord Mayor of London.

High in the south-west tower, above the clock faces, hangs the largest of all the bells, Great Paul, which is rung every weekday for five minutes from one o'clock. It weighs 17 tonnes and is the heaviest bell in Britain. Great Paul was cast in November 1881 by John Taylor & Co of Loughborough who, three years earlier, had cast the cathedral's ring of twelve bells. Transporting it from there to St Paul's was a formidable operation undertaken by a Coventry firm, Coles & Matthews. A strengthened truck was used, pulled by a steam traction engine. Mr Coles, riding his tricycle, supervised the eleven-day journey to the cathedral.

The Dean's Doorway had to be widened to admit Great Paul (below).

The hoisting of the bell up to the clock level of the tower was carried out by a detachment of Royal Engineers and took fifteen hours. The service of dedication took place on Saturday, 3 June 1882. Some ten years later Great Paul was raised to its present position above the clock faces. In 1971 the ringing of this bell was mechanized by the installation of electric motors, paid for by the Friends of St Paul's.

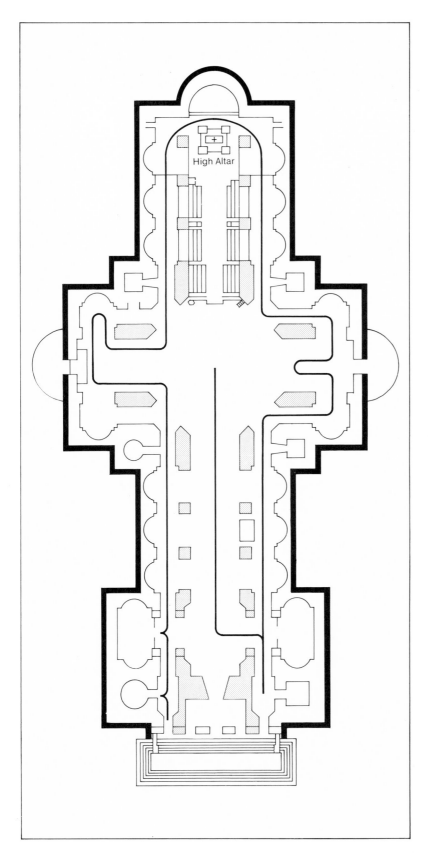

High Altar

The chandelier in the Chapel of St Dunstan (above) was formerly in St Mildred Poultry. The mosaic is by Salviati.

Robert R. Green, Dean's Virger and diarist of St Paul's (right).

A plan of the cathedral floor showing the route taken in the book.

The Cathedral Floor

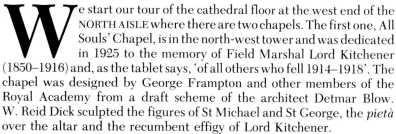

We start our tour of the cathedral floor at the west end of the NORTH AISLE where there are two chapels. The first one, All Souls' Chapel, is in the north-west tower and was dedicated in 1925 to the memory of Field Marshal Lord Kitchener (1850–1916) and, as the tablet says, 'of all others who fell 1914–1918'. The chapel was designed by George Frampton and other members of the Royal Academy from a draft scheme of the architect Detmar Blow. W. Reid Dick sculpted the figures of St Michael and St George, the *pietà* over the altar and the recumbent effigy of Lord Kitchener.

In a recess in the north wall are the Rolls of Honour of the Royal Engineers, of whom Kitchener was Colonel-in-Chief, who died in the two World Wars. The two large silver candlesticks on the altar were wrought from melted-down trophies won by members of the London Rifle Brigade. The colours of the Second Battalion Grenadier Guards, deposited in the cathedral in October 1933, hang opposite the chapel.

Next is a larger chamber, the Chapel of St Dunstan, with a splendid entrance screen carved by Jonathan Maine who was one of Wren's great craftsmen. We shall see his work in many other areas of the cathedral. The first mosaics executed for St Paul's are in this chapel. At the west end is the one by Antonio Salviati which portrays the women at the Sepulchre. This is a memorial to Archdeacon William Hale (1795–1870). The mosaic over the altar is an adaptation of a Raphael fresco by William Richmond. Salviati's work is in the smooth, Venetian style while Richmond employed the earlier method of inserting the tesserae, or cubes of glass, irregularly in the soft cement, leaving spaces between to increase the reflection.

Continuing eastwards we see the first of the many grilles which are set at intervals in the floor. Iron grilles were introduced in 1858 but were replaced by these more decorative brass ones in 1881. For many decades, until hot-water central heating was introduced, the grilles were essential to the heating of the cathedral. Before special services involving processions they are covered over to avoid accidents.

Robert Russell Green, who was a virger for forty-seven years, joined the cathedral staff in 1852. It should be explained here that St Paul's never adopted the spelling 'verger' but retained the original 'virger'. The building was extremely cold in winter with the thermometer inside down to freezing point. In the two-volume transcript of Green's notes and memoranda held in the library, and always referred to as his *Diary*, we read:

December 1858. Various plans for warming the cathedral have been made from time to time. Archdeacon Hale had a sort of waggon drawn about the cathedral floor, filled with red hot coke. But after the Gurney stoves were introduced and placed in different parts of the crypt, the hot air passing through the gratings in the floor, the thermometer reached over sixty degrees in the winter frequently and seldom below.

The Gurney stoves were combustion stoves which had fins cast all round the casing to increase their efficiency. When Hale wrote to Canon Sydney Smith telling him of his earliest scheme, Smith said in his reply: 'You are a romantic Canon to talk about warming St Paul's. The only real way of doing it is to warm the County of Middlesex. . . .'

In the first bay in the north wall are memorials to the artist Lord Leighton (1830–96), President of the Royal Academy in 1878; Archbishop Frederick Temple (1821–1902) and the cavalry dead of the Russian wars 1854–6.

On either side of the Wellington monument are memorial tablets to Field Marshal William Slim (1891–1970) and to the serving members of the Indian Army, 1746–1947. The huge monument to the Duke of Wellington (1769–1852) fills the central bay of the north nave aisle. The painter and sculptor, Alfred Stevens, worked on this monument for twenty years and it was still incomplete at his death in 1875. The figure of the Duke on horseback was sculpted by John Tweed and was added in 1912.

Wellington's funeral carriage, formerly in the crypt, is now at Stratfield Saye House. This model is in the cathedral Library.

The Wellington monument by Alfred Stevens, surmounted by the equestrian statue by John Tweed.

The second bay in the north wall contains the memorial to General Charles Gordon (1833–85), who was killed at Khartoum, and to his brother Sir Henry Gordon (1818–87); and memorials to the generals Herbert Stewart (1843–85) and Arthur Torrens (1809–55). The colours of the Royal Fusiliers (City of London Regiment) hang in this bay over the memorial to the officers and men who died in the Afghan War 1879–80.

In the third bay is the monument by Carlo Marochetti in the form of a double door guarded by two angels. The inscription over the door reads: 'Through the gate of death we pass to our joyful resurrection.' It is a memorial to William Lamb, 2nd Viscount Melbourne (1779–1848), who was Queen Victoria's first Prime Minister, and to his brother Frederick, 3rd Viscount Melbourne (1782–1853), the diplomat. Also here are the memorial to Field Marshal Lord Roberts (1832–1914) and the one to the officers, seamen, marines and boys who died when HMS *Captain* foundered off Finisterre on 7 September 1870.

On both sides of the aisle tablets list the Deans of St Paul's since 1066. Finally at this eastern end, there is the door to the Lord Mayor's Vestry.

The Gate of Death memorial to the Melbourne brothers, William and Frederick, by Marochetti.

Before continuing to the north transept, it is necessary to explain the background to the number and nature of the monuments which will be seen there and on the rest of the tour.

In 1793 war broke out between Britain and France and it lasted, with two brief interludes, until 1815. That conflict included numerous land and sea battles in Europe, the Middle East and North Africa. Concurrent with that bloodshed were the wars in North America, India and South Africa. Throughout most of the nineteenth century there were expeditions to establish British supremacy to places as diverse as Cyprus and Ceylon, Mauritius and Singapore. Between 1793 and 1877 Britain was involved in six Kaffir wars, four Mysore wars, two Burmese wars, two Maratta wars as well as assorted mutinies and rebellions. All this led to numerous deeds of bravery and deaths in battle and created many national heroes.

At the same time British sculpture was entering an extended period of neo-classicism, led by Bacon, Flaxman and Banks, producing life-size, and larger, statues and monuments crowded with laurel leaves and allegorical figures representing qualities such as Honour and Valour.

These two trends coincided with the decision to allow statues in the cathedral. The results may be seen on the cathedral floor, particularly in the transepts where memorials to worthy civilians are far outnumbered by flamboyant monuments to naval and military leaders.

Wellington's funeral procession moving eastwards along Fleet Street.

The statue of the portrait painter and first president of the Royal Academy, Joshua Reynolds (1723–92), by John Flaxman, is at the corner of the NORTH TRANSEPT. The Latin inscription describes him as 'Prince of the painters of his age' and the pedestal on which his left hand rests carries a profile of Michelangelo.

C. R. Cockerell (1788–1863), who was the Cathedral Surveyor from 1819 to 1852, is commemorated by a tablet on the left. Opposite is the life-size terracotta sculpture of the Virgin and Child by Josephena de Vasconcellos, which was presented to the cathedral by Bernard Sunley.

Rising Christ *by Josephena de Vasconcellos in St Bartholomew-the-Great, Smithfield.*

Three years after her Virgin and Child was presented to St Paul's Cathedral Vasconcellos sculpted a statue for St Bartholomew-the-Great. St Bartholomew-the-Great is the church of the priory which was built early in the twelfth century by Rahere, the founder of St Bartholomew's Hospital. From 1115 until his death in 1144 Rahere was a prebendary of St Paul's Cathedral.

We now come to the North Transept Chapel, also known as the Middlesex Chapel. The chairs and kneelers are gifts of the Middlesex Regiment and their regimental colours hang from the walls. There is a key to these colours on the south-west pier. The large marble font is at the west end and in the west bay is the memorial to General Thomas Picton (1758–1815) who was killed at the Battle of Waterloo. This is the most famous work of the sculptor, Sebastian Gahagan, and consists of a bust of Picton surrounded by figures representing Genius, Valour and Victory.

On the left of the north door is the monument of the Scottish hero General Andrew Hay (1762–1814) by Humphrey Hopper. The General is depicted expiring in the arms of Valour with a sentinel grieving on the left and a squad of marching soldiers on the right. The joint memorial by Francis Chantrey to the generals Arthur Gore (d.1814) and John Byne Skerrett (d.1814) is to the right of the door. They were both killed in the disastrous assault on French troops holding the Dutch town of Bergen-op-Zoom on 8 March 1814.

The large marble font, sculpted in 1726–7 by Francis Bird, is now in the Middlesex Chapel.

In this north wall of the chapel there is an ambry, or recess, for the reservation of the Blessed Sacrament. The carved door, depicting a 'Pelican in her Piety', is the work of the present Master Carver of St Paul's, Tony Webb. The fable relates that the female pelican pecks her breast and revives and feeds her young with her own blood; hence the pelican has become, in Christian art, a symbol of charity and an emblem of Jesus Christ.

The moveable altar, with its cylindrical supports of etched glass, was constructed in 1973 and is dedicated to the memory of the Reverend Bernard Spink who died in 1941 after thirty-eight years as a priest in the diocese of London. Behind the altar is a sixteenth-century painting in the manner of Titian entitled *The Virgin and Child with St Luke and Donor*.

Leaving the chapel at the east end, we see on the left the monument by John Bacon Jun. to General Thomas Dundas (1750–94) with many allegorical figures, including Sensibility and the Genius of Britain; while on the pedestal, Britannia is depicted defending Liberty against Fraud and Rebellion. On the right is the memorial to Captain Robert Faulkner, RN (1763–95) by John Rossi.

Turning towards the choir, we pass on the left a curtained-off area, sometimes referred to as the Musicians' Aisle, which contains a tablet listing the organists of St Paul's and memorials to the generals John G. Le Marchant (1766–1812) and Bernard Foord Bowes (d.1812) and to the composers Arthur Sullivan (1842–1900) and John Stainer (1840–1901), who was also the Cathedral Organist from 1872 until 1888.

At the entrance to the NORTH CHOIR AISLE, also known as the Minor Canons' Aisle, stands the statue of Samuel Johnson (1709–84) by John Bacon. This monument, which depicts the great lexicographer, conversationalist and man of letters in Ancient Greek costume, was paid for by public subscription started by the Literary Club, of which Johnson was a founder member along with Joshua Reynolds, Oliver Goldsmith, Edmund Burke and five others. The cost was 1100 guineas and the statue was placed here in February 1796 after being on public view for some time.

First on the left in the north choir aisle is the door to the Minor Canons' Vestry; opposite there is a door inscribed 'Organista' which used to give access to the console of the organ when it was on this north side of the choir. Next there are various displays of books, tapestries and cloths and of the consoles of superseded organs. The memorial screen on the left lists the names of former choristers who died in the two World Wars.

James Boswell wrote in his *Life of Samuel Johnson*:

Having arrived in London late on Friday, the 15th of March 1776, I hastened next morning to wait on Dr Johnson at his house; but found he was removed from Johnson's-court, No. 7, to Bolt-court, No. 8, still keeping to his favourite Fleet-street.

The first of Johnson's three houses in the City, 17 Gough Square, is the only surviving one. It was bought and pre-served as a memorial to Johnson in 1911 by the Liberal politician, Lord Harmsworth of Egham (1869–1948). The house, which is open to the public, is managed by a charitable trust.

The statue of Dr Samuel Johnson by John Bacon (above).

The Cheshire Cheese in Wine Office Court, Fleet Street (right). The tradition is that Johnson, Goldsmith and Boswell frequented this hostelry.

The north transept was severely damaged by a heavy high-explosive bomb on the night of 16/17 April 1941 and the falling debris broke through the floor and demolished the vault over the central bay in the crypt. After the war it was estimated that £100,000 would be required in addition to the compensation due from the War Damage Commission to carry out the necessary repairs.

Canon Alexander, the Cathedral Treasurer, believed that a great organized campaign was not necessary, rather the cathedral should approach the City of London and the money would be forthcoming. He was proved right. Dean Matthews wrote in *A History of St Paul's Cathedral* (1957): 'In a comparatively short time, and without spending a penny on publicity or organisation, more than the sum asked for was contributed, almost entirely from the City.'

The carved panelling opposite, which is in fact the rear of the stalls on the north side of the choir, is the work of Grinling Gibbons, the sculptor and wood carver who was born in Rotterdam of English parents. He came

19

to England as a youth and, after a stay in Yorkshire, settled as a married man in Deptford. The diarist John Evelyn discovered Gibbons in 1671 carving a crucifix in 'a poore solitary thatched house in a field' near Sayes Court, the diarist's family seat at Deptford.

Evelyn took the crucifix to London, showing it to King Charles II and, later, to Christopher Wren and Samuel Pepys. As a result Gibbons was employed on the refurbishing of the chapel at Windsor and, quite extensively as we shall see, in the building of St Paul's.

The ceiling mosaics in the saucer domes by William Richmond show, from west to east, angels on reversed anchors with ships in the background; angels in armour, blowing trumpets; and four angels with sheaves of wheat. The shields, in the same sequence, are of the Glynn family, the Dean and Chapter of St Paul's and the Benyon family. On the western arch Jesus is portrayed with sheaves of corn and on the eastern arch is Orpheus with his lute.

The marble statue, *Mother and Child*, was specially created by Henry Moore for St Paul's and is on permanent loan from the Henry Moore Foundation. The sculpture, carved in travertine marble, was described by a member of the Cathedrals Advisory Commission for England as having 'an elemental and yet eminently approachable quality, expressive of motherhood and compassion'.

At the eastern end of this aisle is the Chapel of the Modern Martyrs, which commemorates Anglican martyrs since 1850. All the known names are recorded in a book which is displayed in a glass-topped marble casket. The altar was previously in the Jesus Chapel, which is now the American Memorial Chapel, and the crucifix was part of the Victorian reredos damaged by a bomb in 1940 and subsequently removed.

On the right is the SANCTUARY SCREEN, which is predominantly by Jean Tijou, the French smith who was responsible for most of the ornamental ironwork in the cathedral. He had first been employed by Wren in the building of Hampton Court and it was there that he set up his workshop. This screen and gates and those in the opposite aisle are considered by experts to be Tijou's finest work in England.

At eye level there are representations of Old Testament prophets wrought into the ironwork pillars and above each pillar is a large, handsome candlestick. All this was removed from its original position across the west end of the choir in 1890 and the date appears at the top of the screen. That and other additions to Tijou's work were designed by the architects George F. Bodley and Thomas Garner and were made at the ironworks of Messrs Barketin and Krall at Lamberhurst, Sussex. In the 1960s the sanctuary screen and gates were refurbished with gold-leaf decoration.

We pass through the gates and enter the small chapel in the apse which is now the AMERICAN MEMORIAL CHAPEL. Two architects, Godfrey Allen and Stephen Dykes Bower, designed the restoration of the whole of the war-damaged east end of the cathedral, including this chapel.

On the right there is a gold and glass case on a marble pedestal which contains the Roll of Honor listing the name, rank and service of some 28,000 members of the American forces who lost their lives in Britain, or on active service from British bases, during the Second World War. The roll was prepared by members of General Eisenhower's staff and consists of 500 pages of illuminated manuscript bound in a red leather volume. It was handed over by the General to the Dean and Chapter of St Paul's on Independence Day, 4 July 1951.

The American Memorial Chapel showing the altar, the south stalls and the Roll of Honor.

Seven years later the chapel was completed and the service of dedication on 26 November 1958 was attended by HM The Queen, Vice-President Nixon and twelve next-of-kin representing the many thousands of bereaved relatives.

The three stained glass windows in the chapel are the only coloured windows on the cathedral floor. They were designed by Brian Thomas and made at the Whitefriars Studios. The designs represent the service, sacrifice and resurrection of the faithful soldier. The borders carry the insignia of the states and territories of the USA and of the US army and navy. There are six oak stalls at either side of the chapel altar with medallion portraits of Queen Elizabeth II and President Eisenhower, and of the two architects, on the inner and outer ends respectively. The panelled walls have limewood carvings, by George Haslop, of American birds, flowers and fruits. On the altar are a tall silver and gold cross and two candlesticks. The altar rails are of wrought iron, decorated with gold-leaf to match the sanctuary screen and gates. Some significant dates in the history of St Paul's and of the USA are worked into the rails.

The floor is of black and white Italian marble and has a design of two five-pointed stars – the symbol of the Allied Forces in the Second World War. The money to cover the cost of the chapel came from British men, women and children; all offers of financial help from elsewhere were refused. The following inscription is inlaid around the perimeter of the floor:

TO THE AMERICAN DEAD OF THE SECOND WORLD WAR
FROM THE PEOPLE OF BRITAIN

The architect Godfrey Allen, who at the time of writing is 93 years old, was Surveyor to the Fabric of St Paul's from 1931 to 1956. After the Second World War he restored a number of bomb-damaged churches in the City, including St Dunstan-in-the-West; St Bride's, Fleet Street; St Mary Abchurch and St Giles, Cripplegate.

At a Court of Common Council meeting on 12 June 1945 General Dwight D. Eisenhower, Supreme Commander of the Allied Forces in Europe, was admitted to the Honorary Freedom of the City and was presented with a Sword of Honour. In his address the Chamberlain said: 'General Eisenhower cannot be in any doubt about the emotions he has aroused among all classes in this country, and yet there is one welcome without which his reception in this country cannot be complete – the welcome of this ancient City. . . .'

Fourteen years later, as President Eisenhower, he paid a brief visit to London. Again crowds of City workers and sightseers cheered him as he was driven to St Paul's to visit the American Memorial Chapel. There, he was escorted by Dr J. W. C. Wand, former Bishop of London, and Lord Baillieu, the City banker and industrialist, Chairman of the Memorial Chapel fund.

In a letter to Lord Baillieu, dated 31 August 1959, President Eisenhower said:

I cannot adequately tell you the emotions that crossed my mind and heart this morning when finally I had the privilege of seeing the American Memorial Chapel at St Paul's Cathedral. It is even more impressive and beautiful than I had visualized.

The eighteenth-century Bavarian crucifix and candlesticks in the Lady Chapel, presented on behalf of the West German people by President Heuss (right).

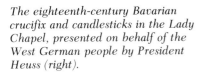

City crowds cheering General Eisenhower on his way to the Mansion House after receiving the Freedom of the City (left).

Passing through to the SOUTH CHOIR AISLE (or Dean's Aisle) we come to the Lady Chapel, which was created as recently as 1959. Although there is no special enclosure to this chapel, its furnishings and ornaments are of particular interest. The oak altar table is the cathedral's original High Altar and the statue of the Blessed Virgin and Child was part of the Victorian reredos. The statue is framed by a section of Wren's organ screen which was removed from the choir entrance in 1859. The wooden crucifix and candlesticks on the altar are of eighteenth-century Bavarian make. President Theodor Heuss of West Germany presented them to St Paul's during his state visit to Britain in October 1958.

The mosaics in each of the three saucer domes in this aisle depict four angels: in the first they are shown carrying staves and fruit, in the second they are playing violins and in the third they are shown with scrolls and castles. The shields in these domes carry Masonic emblems, the arms of the Dean and Chapter and the arms of the City respectively.

23

Donne dressed in his shroud (far left). This effigy by Nicholas Stone was the only figure from Old St Paul's to survive intact.

Thornycroft's handsome statue of Mandell Creighton (left). The pediment epitaph reads: 'He tried to write true history.'

Continuing down the aisle, on the left is the effigy of Charles James Blomfield (1786–1857) who was not only a distinguished classical scholar but also a founder Fellow of the Royal Statistical Society. Blomfield was Bishop of London from 1829 until 1856. He created a fund for the building and endowment of churches for the expanding population of London. The fund prospered and the Bishop himself gave generously to it from his own extremely high salary of over £20,000 a year. During the twenty-seven years of his episcopate he consecrated 200 new churches.

This effigy was sculpted by George Richmond who was the father of Sir William Richmond, the designer of most of the St Paul's mosaics. Sir Reginald Blomfield, who created the Paul's Cross Memorial in 1910, was Bishop Blomfield's grandson.

Next, on the right, is the virgers' office; while on the left is the upright effigy of the most famous Dean of St Paul's, John Donne (1573–1631). Donne, who was born a Catholic, adopted the Anglican faith in adult life. He tried a number of professions before being ordained priest in 1614 at the age of 41. He wrote passionate love poems, *Songs and Sonnets*, as well as the *Satires*, *Elegies* and *Divine Poems*. Although many of his poems circulated widely among his friends, few of them were published during his lifetime.

Donne's prose works include *Pseudo-Martyr* (1610), a polemic against those English Catholics who refused to take the oath of allegiance to James I; and *Biathanatos* (pub. 1644), in which he discussed suicide and concluded that, in some circumstances, it may not be a sin. Donne was a great preacher and his published *Sermons* and *Devotions* are still often quoted from, if not so often read, today.

Opposite the Donne effigy is William Hamo Thornycroft's striking bronze statue of the historian and prelate, Dr Mandell Creighton. After becoming the first professor of ecclesiastical history at Cambridge in 1884, Creighton was successively Bishop of Peterborough (1891) and Bishop of London (1896). The entrance to the stairs up to the organ console is just past this statue.

Next on the left is the Prebendaries' Vestry, on either side of which are some relics from Jerusalem affixed to the wall. They include a piece of stone from Solomon's Temple and a fragment from Herod's Temple. The latter was brought here by Canon Liddon after his visit to the Holy Land in 1886. Finally in this aisle, on the left-hand side, there is the door to the Dean's Vestry.

At the corner of the SOUTH TRANSEPT stands the first statue to be erected in St Paul's – that of the Dissenter and philanthropist, John Howard (1726–90). He is represented in Roman costume, treading on fetters. In his right hand he holds a key and in his left a scroll on which can be read: 'Plan for the Improvement of Prisons and Hospitals'.

In 1756 Howard himself suffered imprisonment in Brest after being captured by a French privateer. After his appointment as High-Sheriff of Bedfordshire, he realized that many people were unjustly held in prison and that prison conditions were appalling. He then assumed the role of inspector of prisons at home and abroad and worked without the support of any government or charitable agency. The Howard League for Penal Reform is named after him.

The base panel to John Howard's monument depicts him succouring prisoners.

The monument is by John Bacon and the eulogistic inscription was composed by Samuel Whitbread, MP. Here is one sentence from it: 'In every part of the civilised world, which he traversed to reduce the sum of human misery, from the throne to the dungeon, his name was mentioned with respect, gratitude and admiration.'

Next is the memorial tablet to the explorer, Captain Robert Falcon Scott, RN (1868–1912) and to his companions who died with him on the return journey from the South Pole.

Over the doorway to the crypt there is a monument to General Robert Ross (1766–1814) who was killed in a battle near the city of Baltimore, USA, during the war of 1812. It was during the attack on Baltimore that Francis Scott Key composed *The Star-Spangled Banner*, now the US national anthem. At a similar height on the pier opposite is a panel commemorating Colonel Henry Cadogan (1780–1813), by Sir Francis Chantrey. He was killed fighting with Wellington's forces at the Battle of Vittoria and is depicted being carried, mortally wounded, to a hill from where he might witness the outcome of the fight.

Over on the left is the statue by William Behnes of General John T. Jones (1797–1843) of the Royal Engineers; while opposite is the monument of Sir Henry Montgomery Lawrence (1806–57) who was killed defending Lucknow during the Indian Mutiny.

Two naval heroes are commemorated on the left: first is Admiral Earl Howe (1726–99) and the monument is by the artist, designer and sculptor, John Flaxman. In a long naval career Howe's most famous achievement was victory over the French fleet off Ushant on 'the glorious first of June' 1794. The second monument is to the memory of Admiral Lord Collingwood (1750–1810) who was Vice-Admiral of the Blue – that is, Nelson's second-in-command – at the Battle of Trafalgar. The memorial was sculpted by Sir Richard Westmacott and depicts a ship nearing the English coast with the body of Collingwood stretched on the deck, shrouded in colours won from French and Spanish vessels. Father Thames and the spirits of other rivers are in attendance.

The pediment of the Royal Exchange shows Commerce with a Lord Mayor and representations of trading countries and regions.

The first building of the Royal Exchange was modelled by Sir Thomas Gresham on the Antwerp bourse and the first meeting of merchants was held there on 22 December 1568. It was on a visit to the Exchange by Queen Elizabeth I in 1571 that she commanded it should be called the Royal Exchange. Gresham entrusted the Royal Exchange to the City Corporation and the Mercers' Company.

It was destroyed in 1666 in the Great Fire and the new building, by Edward Jarman, was also destroyed by fire in 1838. The present building is the work of the architect, Sir William Tite, and was constructed during the years 1842–4. The pediment sculpture was carved by Sir Richard Westmacott whose work can be seen throughout the cathedral.

The memorial to the painter, J. M. W. Turner (1775–1851) is next on this side; while against the opposite pier is the more elaborate statue of General Lord Heathfield (1717–90). Heathfield is famous for his successful defence of Gibraltar, against the combined French and Spanish forces, for four years from 1779 to 1783. The statue was sculpted by J. C. F. Rossi.

Just before we reach the south transept door we see another Westmacott sculpture – the joint memorial to General Edward Pakenham (1778–1815) and General Samuel Gibbs (d.1815), his second-in-command. Both were killed in the disastrous attack on New Orleans on 8 January 1815 during the war of 1812. The tragic irony was that a peace treaty ending the war had been signed at Ghent on 24 December 1814 but it was not ratified by the US Senate until 16 February 1815. Over 3000 of Pakenham's men were killed with him in the battle. The south transept door is a handsome construction from parts of the organ screen which was taken down from across the west end of the choir in May 1860.

Opposite the south door stands another monument sculpted by Rossi. This is to the Marquis Cornwallis, Governor-General of Bengal (1738–1805), and consists of a central statue of the Marquis in the robes of a Knight of the Garter, surrounded by figures representing Britannia, the Ganges and another Indian river, the Bhagirathi. Marquis Cornwallis died at Ghazipur while on his way to assume command of the army in the field.

The monument to Lord Cornwallis by J. C. F. Rossi.

Frank Salisbury's painting of the arrival of King George V and Queen Mary for the Jubilee thanksgiving service, 6 May 1935.

Some 12 metres (40 feet) high above the Cornwallis monument is the Flaxman memorial to Captain R. Willet Miller, RN (1762–99), who was killed in an explosion aboard the *Theseus* off the coast of Acre. A representation of the *Theseus* appears on the monument.

Also by Flaxman is the next memorial – the elaborate monument to Admiral Viscount Nelson (1758–1805). On a high pedestal, Nelson is depicted leaning on an anchor with a coiled rope at his feet. The lack of his right arm is concealed by a cloak draped over his shoulder. On the pedestal are carved representations of the North Sea, the Baltic Sea, the Nile and the Mediterranean. On one side is a lion couchant and on the other Britannia is pointing Nelson out to two young sailors.

The tablet above the Nelson statue is to the memory of Captain George Hardinge, RN (1781–1808), who was killed aboard his ship the *San Fiorenzo* in a battle against the French cruiser *Piedmontaise* off the coast of Ceylon.

The statue by Francis Chantrey of General Robert Gillespie (1766–1814) is over on the left-hand side. Next to it is the memorial to the colonial troops who died in the South African War, 1899–1902. The tablet, which is

Their Majesties the
King and Queen
entering the Great West Door

with Praise

headed: AUSTRALIA · CANADA · CEYLON · NEW ZEALAND · SOUTH AFRICA · carries a dedication which reads: 'To the Glory of God and to the undying honour of those 4300 sons of Britain beyond the seas who gave their lives for love of the Mother Land in the South African War 1899–1902.'

The large bronze sculpture above the tablet depicts an angel lifting Christ from the cross, symbolizing salvation through suffering. The monument is signed and dated on the tablet: 'Louise 1904'. The sculptress 'Louise' was the Princess Louise, the fourth daughter of Queen Victoria, who became the Duchess of Argyll. Princess Louise had literary and artistic talents and her circle of friends included the sculptors J. E. Boehm, Alfred Gilbert and Lawrence Alma-Tadema.

On the piers in this part of the transept hang a group of flags. They are the Banners of the Dominions of Australia, New Zealand and Canada, along with the Banner of the United Kingdom. The Dean and Chapter of the cathedral had them placed here in 1935 to commemorate the Silver Jubilee of His Majesty King George V and Queen Mary, an occasion beautifully captured by Frank Salisbury's painting.

Next is the statue of General John Moore (1761–1809) by John Bacon Jun. After a long retreat in winter from Astorga to Coruña during the Peninsular War, Moore's forces inflicted a heavy defeat on the French army there on 16 January 1809. He was killed by grapeshot at the moment of victory. The monument depicts the General being lowered into his grave by figures representing Valour and Victory. The spirit of Spain is shown planting a standard over the tomb.

In 1817 the poem *The Burial of Sir John Moore* by the Irish poet, the Reverend Charles Wolfe, was published. It opens with the stirring lines:

Not a drum was heard, not a funeral note,
    As his corpse to the rampart we hurried. . .

This poem was memorized and recited by many generations of British schoolchildren.

Opposite the Moore monument is the statue of Captain William Hoste RN; while on the left there is a memorial to a great civilian – the eminent surgeon, Sir Astley Cooper (1768–1841). Cooper was not only surgeon to, successively, George IV, William IV and Queen Victoria, but also treated the humblest patients as surgeon to Guy's Hospital, London, for forty-two years.

Finally, on the left-hand side are the monuments to General Ralph Abercromby (1734–1801) and to Admiral Lord Lyons (1790–1858). The inscription on the latter monument simply states: 'Erected by his friends and admirers.'

The Abercromby monument, on the other hand, has an extremely lengthy inscription describing both his career and the circumstances of his fatal wounding at the Battle of Aboukir and his subsequent death on board the *Foudroyant*. Westmacott sculpted the monument which shows the General falling from his horse into the arms of a Scottish soldier. A fallen French soldier lies under the horse's hooves. On either side of the plinth there is a sphinx, symbolizing Egypt, the country where Abercromby met his death.

Opposite the Admiral Lyons monument is the statue by William Behnes of Dr William Babington (1756–1833), the physician and mineralogist, who is generally credited with founding the Geological Society.

A little further on, in a glass case in a niche, are the volumes comprising the Roll of Honour of the 33,000 members of the Merchant Navy and the fishing fleets who died while serving during the Second World War.

High above the Merchant Navy memorial there is a monument to General Isaac Brock (1769–1812) by Westmacott. Brock was killed defending Queenstown in Canada against the American attack led by Stephen Van Rensselaer on 13 October 1812. Brock is depicted, fatally wounded, in the arms of a brother officer, with a North American Indian standing by in mourning attitude.

On the corner, before you turn left into the SOUTH AISLE, stands the memorial to Sir William Jones (1746–94) by John Bacon. Jones was a high court judge in Calcutta where he died. He was also an orientalist, poet and linguist and there are many allegorical references to his scholarship carved on the monument.

The headquarters of the East India Company, Leadenhall Street, pictured in 1802.

After Robert Clive assumed control of Bengal in 1765, the government of India was in the hands of the East India Company. The British government gradually took over various aspects of administration until, in 1858, all the Company's possessions were transferred to the crown and Victoria was proclaimed Empress of India. Sir William Jones worked extremely hard during his ten years in Bengal. He studied and published works on Hindu and Mohammedan law; he was the first European to master Sanskrit and translated many oriental works; and he founded the Asiatic Society of Bengal. In recognition of all these efforts the directors of the East India Company voted the necessary money for the memorial to Jones in St Paul's.

Inside the painting frame:

THE LIGHT
OF THE WORLD

BEHOLD I STAND AT THE DOOR AND KNOCK IF ANY MAN
HEAR MY VOICE AND OPEN THE DOOR I WILL COME
IN TO HIM AND WILL SVP WITH HIM AND HE WITH ME.

The Light of the World *by William Holman Hunt, completed in 1904.*

    The Bishops of London since the year 314 are listed on four tablets around the corner near the entrance to the stairs to the galleries.

    On the left is the monument by Carlo Marochetti to Captain Granville Loch (1813–53) who was killed during the Second Burmese War while Captain of HMS *Winchester*. Next to it is the splendid memorial to the Captain of HMS *Majestic*, George Blagdon Westcott (1743–98), who was killed during the Battle of the Nile. The bas-relief carvings on the base depict a sea battle, the exploding of the French ship *L'Orient* and the Egyptian shore with sphinxes and palm trees. The sculptor was Thomas Banks. A third naval hero, Captain Edmund Lyons (1819–55), son of Admiral Lord Lyons, is commemorated by a tablet.

Holman Hunt's The Eve of St Agnes, *one of the many Pre-Raphaelite paintings in the Guildhall Art Gallery.*

32

Next on this side is one of the most celebrated religious pictures ever painted: William Holman Hunt's *The Light of the World*. Thousands of reproductions of it appear every year on postcards, posters, slides and calendars.

This nearly life-size painting 2.33 × 1.28 metres (7 feet 8 inches × 4 feet 2½ inches) is the third and largest version of *The Light of the World* which Holman Hunt produced. The first, which was completed in 1853 and measures 1.25 metres × 596 millimetres (4 feet 1⅜ inches × 1 foot 11½ inches), is at Keble College, Oxford. In 1857 a small replica of the picture 497 × 261 millimetres (1 foot 7⅝ inches × 10 5/16 inches) was painted in Holman Hunt's studio. It was acquired in 1912 by the City of Manchester and is still exhibited in the City Art Gallery.

The painting seen here was completed in 1904, some fifty years after the Keble College version. It was bought by the wealthy shipowner and social investigator, Charles Booth (1840–1916), who sent it on an exhibition tour of the British Commonwealth to Canada, Australia, New Zealand and South Africa. Booth then presented the picture to St Paul's Cathedral. It was received at a formal ceremony on 5 June 1908, attended by the 81-year-old artist, William Holman Hunt.

Holman Hunt was one of the founder members of the group of artists who called themselves the Pre-Raphaelite Brotherhood (1848). There are several Pre-Raphaelite paintings in the City of London's Guildhall Art Gallery collection, including works by John Everett Millais, D. G. Rossetti, J. R. Herbert, W. S. Burton and Holman Hunt.

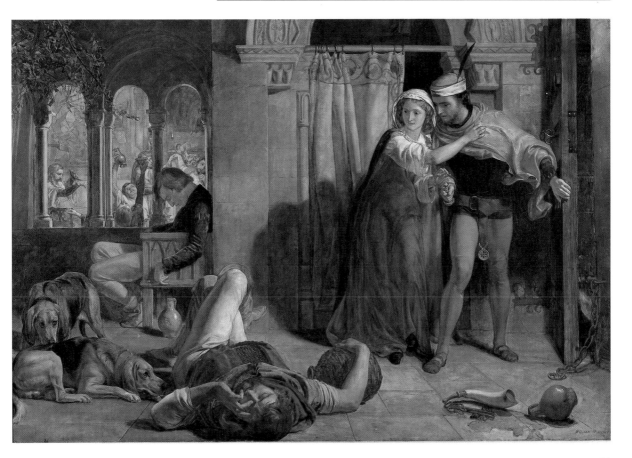

In the bay next to *The Light of the World* is the monument to Thomas Fanshaw Middleton (1769–1822), the first Anglican Bishop of India. The memorial, by J. G. Lough, depicts Bishop Middleton blessing two Indian children kneeling before him. Another monument by Thomas Banks comes next. This is a memorial to Captain Richard Rundle Burges (1755–97) who was killed commanding HMS *Ardent* at the Battle of Camperdown.

Thomas Middleton was a scholar at Christ's Hospital from 1779 to 1789 when he entered Pembroke College, Cambridge. Christ's Hospital, the famous Bluecoat school which was founded by Edward VI in 1553, was then in Newgate Street in the City of London. Middleton loved the school which he described as 'the noblest institution in the world'. His particular friends there included Charles Lamb and Samuel Taylor Coleridge.

In 1902 the school removed to Horsham in West Sussex. A farewell service was held in St Paul's Cathedral at which the Archbishop of Canterbury, Dr Frederick Temple, preached the sermon. On Tuesday, 19 May 1953 staff, pupils and many former pupils of Christ's Hospital ('Old Blues') returned to the City for a thanksgiving service in St Paul's to mark the fourth centenary of the founding of the school (1553–1953).

On the opposite side of the aisle is the mobile organ known as 'Willis on Wheels'. It was built by Henry Willis and, as Virger Green tells us, it was first used at the Communion Service on Wednesday, 21 December 1881. It was rebuilt in 1928 and re-erected in the north choir aisle. After the chancel was closed in October 1940 because of bomb damage, this organ was removed to the nave and used for all cathedral services as well as for weekly recitals throughout the war.

On the left we come to the Chapel of the Order of St Michael and St George. This was originally the Consistory – the Ecclesiastical Court of the Diocese of London. From 1878 the Wellington monument was housed here until its removal to the north aisle in 1894. The font was then installed and the chapel became the cathedral Baptistry.

In 1901 Archdeacon William Sinclair, a Canon of St Paul's, suggested that this south-west chapel should be 'adapted to the special uses of the Order of St Michael and St George'. The Order, which was founded in 1818, is awarded for services rendered in overseas territories and foreign affairs.

Agreement was reached between the Chancellor of the Order and the Dean and Chapter of St Paul's in 1902. Somers Clarke, the architect to the cathedral, was appointed to design the chapel. On 12 June 1906 the Chapel of St Michael and St George was dedicated by the Prelate of the Order, Bishop Henry Montgomery, in the presence of the Sovereign of the Order, King Edward VII, and the Grand Master, the Prince of Wales. Addressing the hundreds of Knights and Companions of the Order, the Prelate said: 'You who represent the best of the Anglo-Saxon race at work beyond the seas, are now made the guardians of the West Door of the cathedral, in place of the Duke of Wellington.'

The panels on the south wall of the chapel are a memorial to Bishop Montgomery who died in 1932; incidentally, there is a memorial plaque in the crypt to the Bishop's son, Field-Marshal Viscount Montgomery of Alamein (1887–1976).

Somers Clarke's designs for the roof panels included moulded shields of the arms of King Edward VII, the Prince of Wales and the then Chancellor of the Order, Sir Robert Herbert. The teak stalls were made in

Willis on Wheels: this small but powerful instrument was rebuilt in 1968 by Noel Mander who also made it moveable.

The west end of the Chapel of St Michael and St George with the Royal Throne and Knights Grand Cross banners.

1903 by J. E. Knox; while the Royal Throne, which is opposite the altar, incorporated some Grinling Gibbons's work formerly in the Choir – the four cherubs supporting the consoles of the canopy.

A statue of St George surmounts the reredos and a representation of St Michael trampling the seven deadly sins is set in the middle. This latter sculpture, which was added in 1970, was executed by Edwin Russell. The carved screen at the entrance is by Jonathan Maine and the iron railings are the work of one of Wren's smiths, Thomas Robinson.

Leaving the chapel and continuing westward along the aisle, we come to a memorial plaque on the left-hand wall to the Coldstream Guards who died in the South African War 1899–1902. Immediately past this memorial is a door which gives access to the south-west tower.

Here at the entrance we are, of course, well above ground level. Once through the door the steps down lead to the stone and black marble floor, laid in the design of a large star, and to the Dean's Doorway, the attractive outside of which will be discussed during the tour of the environs. But the eye is immediately caught by the lovely spiral of steps which sweeps up the tower to the triforium level. This spectacular construction, known as

The Geometrical Staircase, designed by Wren and built and carved by William Kempster with ironwork by Jean Tijou.

the Geometrical Staircase, or the Dean's Staircase, was designed by Wren and built by William Kempster. Each of the stone steps is set into the wall only a few inches and there is no newel post to support them. From the top the weight at each stage is carried to the next one below, and so on down to the base.

A door at the top leads to the south aisle of the triforium, which is the Library Aisle. Wren designed two libraries: this one and another directly opposite on the north side of the triforium. The Building Accounts of the time refer to both rooms as 'the Library' but, although the north library did contain books for some years during the nineteenth century, these have long been removed and it is now known as the 'Trophy Room'.

A door on the right in the south aisle leads into the LIBRARY. The chamber, which is directly above the Chapel of St Michael and St George, has remained virtually unchanged since its completion in 1709. The woodblock floor by Charles Hopson, the carved brackets under the gallery by Jonathan Maine, the stone pilasters carved by William Kempster on the gallery and the oak presses in which the books are shelved, are all in their original state.

Very few books survived from Old St Paul's and the new library was built up around three main acquisitions. First and most important was the bequest of Henry Compton, Bishop of London at the start of rebuilding and at the completion of the new cathedral. He left half his personal library – 1892 volumes – to St Paul's and the books were received in 1715, two years after Compton's death. A further 1511 volumes were added when the libraries of the Reverend Thomas Mangey and of his son, the Reverend John Mangey, were acquired in 1783.

The library is now rich in rare books, particularly Bibles, New Testaments, concordances and commentaries, service books, liturgical books and rituals. In addition there is a great deal of material which is principally of interest to researchers, who are admitted by appointment: Paul's Cross sermons, early St Paul's Cathedral sermons, early tracts and pamphlets and volumes of manuscript music, especially compositions by St Paul's organists. The library stock is currently being cleaned, checked and re-catalogued; it is now apparent that most of the books require rebinding.

The handsome chamber is long overdue for cleaning and redecorating and the gallery is in urgent need of repair.

In 1980 the cathedral manuscripts were deposited in the Guildhall Library where they are stored in temperature- and humidity-controlled conditions. There they are conserved and made available to researchers by the library's archivists, who also deal with all the correspondence connected with the St Paul's archives.

At the same time the plans and drawings were also transferred to the appropriate department of the Guildhall Library. The Reference Services staff undertake research on behalf of the Dean and Chapter and other members of the Foundation and will accept any postal enquiries received by the cathedral library which may be outside its scope.

Two of the eight stone pilasters on the Library gallery carved by William Kempster (above).

The Library with a portrait of Bishop Compton and, above, Canon Sydney Smith. The carved brackets are by Jonathan Maine (below).

To return to the cathedral floor and the south aisle: there is another memorial tablet to the Coldstream Guards opposite the geometrical staircase door. This one commemorates those who died at the Battle of Inkerman in 1854 during the Crimean War. The tablet was sculpted by Carlo Marochetti, who also executed the Melbourne monument in the north aisle.

Retracing our steps eastward into the cathedral we turn into the vestibule and see, on the right, the Friend's Table from where the special tours of the cathedral, conducted by the Friends of St Paul's, start. Set in the pavement of the vestibule, at the entrance to the nave, is the memorial to the members of St Paul's Watch. It reads:

Remember Men and Women of St Paul's Watch
who by the Grace of God saved this Cathedral
from destruction in war 1939–1945.

At the outbreak of the Second World War the Surveyor to the Fabric, Godfrey Allen, asked the Secretary of the Royal Institute of British Architects to appeal for volunteers to act as fire fighters during the hours of darkness in St Paul's. As a result some forty helpers, mostly architects, were added to the sixty volunteers from the cathedral staff. How the Watch was organized and how it 'saved this Cathedral from destruction' is explained in Dean Matthews's book *St Paul's Cathedral in Wartime 1939–1954* (Hutchinson, 1946).

On 24 October 1945 the Dean and Chapter gave a dinner to members of the Watch in Goldsmiths' Hall. Dr Matthews, in proposing a toast to them, said that they were a motley crew composed of artists, architects, businessmen, students, professors and postmen, as well as clerics. We might add that at least one, the late Sir John Betjeman, was a poet. Nor were they all British. 'It is perhaps a fact of symbolical significance', said the Dean, 'that St Paul's was defended also by Americans, Dutchmen and Czechs.'

City air-raid wardens and others engaged on rescue work in Aldersgate Street to the north-east of the cathedral (above).

Members of St Paul's Watch on the steps to the galleries (left).

Wings for Victory, *a painting by Frank E. Beresford in the cathedral Choir School (right).*

While carrying out their duties the members of St Paul's Watch frequently discussed how they might maintain their links with the cathedral when peace had returned. Soon after the end of hostilities the suggestion was made that they should form themselves into the Society of Friends of St Paul's. This was not, however, immediately well received by the Chapter. Fears of interference with the administration of the cathedral were eventually overcome though, and in April 1952 at a meeting in the crypt the Society of Friends of St Paul's was formed. Queen Elizabeth The Queen Mother consented to be patron and the joint presidents were, ex officio, the Bishop of London and the Lord Mayor.

Since then the Friends of St Paul's have gone from strength to strength. Both their gifts to the cathedral and their daily help over the years have been extraordinarily generous. There is an annual festival service for them in the cathedral attended by The Queen Mother, and often by the Lord Mayor and the Bishop of London. A reception is held afterwards in the crypt.

The popular identification of St Paul's with national survival during the Second World War led to the choice of this site for the City's 'Wings for Victory' week campaign in March 1943. The various 'weeks' were intended to boost sales of National Savings Bonds.

The splendid view down the nave to the High Altar showing the stained glass windows of the American Memorial Chapel.

At the entrance to the NAVE there are two large, bronze candlesticks. The one on the north side has a plate inscribed: 'To the glory of God and in memory of the Reverend Thomas Bayles Murray, Prebendary of St Paul's Cathedral, this candelabrum is presented by his son T. Douglas Murray in 1899.' The sculpting was done by Henry Pegram in 1898 and two casts were made, this and the one on the south side, by the firm of Hollinshead & Burton at its Thames Ditton foundry.

From this position there is an uninterrupted view down the nave, through the dome area to the choir ceiling and the High Altar. Above the arches of the nave bays can be seen the railings of the triforium, or gallery, which is over the north and south aisles, and the St Dunstan's and St Michael and St George Chapels, with a connecting balcony over part of the vestibule. If we turn to look at that balcony we can see the iron railings which were the work of Jean Tijou. The rest of the triforium railings were designed and donated by Somers Clarke, architect to the cathedral from 1897 to 1906. There is a bronze bust of Clarke in the library by the man responsible for the equestrian part of the Wellington monument, John Tweed.

Excluding the vestibule, the nave consists of three bays on either side, the piers of which have a pilaster at each corner and one on the inward-looking face, with Corinthian capitals ornamented with acanthus. We walk down the length of the nave, under the three saucer domes, to the eastern end.

The City Corporation provided the lighting seen in the photograph and subsequently set up the present permanent system of floodlights for the cathedral.

St Paul's floodlit on Victory in Europe night, 8 May 1945.

41

We are now in the DOME AREA. The eight great piers support the weight of the dome – some 64,000 tonnes. That they still do so despite the wartime bombing of the chancel and the north transept, is due to work which was started in 1913 and finished in June 1930. According to Canon Alexander: 'This colossal work was nothing less than that of solidifying and restoring the whole central structure and particularly the great piers that carry the overpowering weight of the Dome. . . .' (*The Safety of St Paul's*, 1930)

An engineering survey by Sir Francis Fox in 1913 reported that iron clamps and ties, which had been used in many areas contrary to Wren's instructions, were badly rusted; that the pier cores were filled with rubble and that many stones were broken and needed replacing. Restoration work started immediately on the south-west pier and continued slowly until 1925 when it was decided to close the dome and choir areas so that the process could be speeded up.

In June 1930 the work was finished and the cathedral was reopened with a thanksgiving service. The operations carried out included the injection of liquid cement under pressure into each pier; replacing broken masonry; removing iron ties and clamps and substituting steel ones and placing a steel chain around the dome.

Some eleven years after the start of restoration work on the dome the City Surveyor inspected the work in progress and his reaction caused a sharp rift in the relations between the Corporation and St Paul's: he drew up and despatched a Dangerous Structure Notice. It was dated 24 December 1924 and, inevitably, was frequently referred to bitterly as 'the City's Christmas present'.

The feelings of the then Dean, Dr W. R. Inge, are recorded in his *Diary of a Dean*. He wrote:

The City Surveyor, a person named Todd, has served us with a notice that St Paul's is 'a dangerous structure', and must be closed. In view of the expert advice on which we rely, this is an act of insolent rudeness. The Lord Mayor and both the Sheriffs are Roman Catholics, but I have no reason to suppose that they will support Mr Todd.

The hurt remained for as long as those involved lived. Twenty-one years after the event, in September 1945 Canon Alexander addressed a meeting of architects and surveyors and recalled that the Dangerous Structure Notice had been delivered to his house on Christmas Eve. It had been produced, he declared, by 'an official of megalomaniac tendencies, who had never made a proper examination of the building'. He also insisted that the closing of the dome and choir areas at the beginning of 1925 was not a consequence of receiving the notice but a coincidence and that there had never been any danger to the public.

Although this incident caused some bad feeling on both sides, it was not of any great significance in the context of the traditional close relations between the cathedral and the City. Evidence of the strength of that relationship appeared just fifteen days after the date of the Dangerous Structure Notice. *The Times* of 8 January 1925 published an appeal for funds to enable repairs to continue, issued jointly by the Dean and Chapter of St Paul's and the Lord Mayor of London.

If we now look upwards and around we see first of all the eight main arches which transfer the thrust of the dome to the piers. Each arch has a massive keystone, carved by Caius Gabriel Cibber, father of the actor, playwright and Poet Laureate, Colley Cibber. More work by C. G. Cibber can be seen on the exterior of the building.

The smooth, flat mosaic work in the spandrels between the arches was done by Salviati from the designs of other artists as follows: St Matthew and St John by G. F. Watts, St Mark and St Luke by A. Britton and the four prophets, Isaiah, Jeremiah, Ezekiel and Daniel, by Alfred Stevens.

The more brilliant mosaics in the quarter domes are by William Richmond, whose work we have already seen in the St Dunstan's Chapel and the choir aisles. The sequence of the four scenes depicted runs anti-clockwise, starting at the north-east quarter with Christ enthroned on the cross as the tree of life, based on Revelation 22: 1–2; then His appearance,

A view of the inside of the dome showing the statues of the Church Fathers and Thornhill's paintings.

entombment and resurrection; these last three being based on I Corinthians 15: 3–6. These saucer dome mosaics were paid for by livery companies. Richmond's series of mosaics here and in the choir and its aisles was started in 1891 and completed in 1907.

Above the main arches is the Whispering Gallery which has the acoustic peculiarity its name implies: a whisper against the blank, circular wall or 'drum' can be heard at the opposite side, some 42.6 metres (140 feet) away. The statues in the niches above the drum are of four Fathers of the Western Church – Ambrose, Augustine, Jerome and Gregory – and four of the Eastern Church – Athanasius, Basil, Gregory of Nazianzus and Chrysostom.

The inner dome is decorated with eight monochrome frescos depicting events in the life of St Paul. They were painted in 1715 by James Thornhill and repainted during the years 1853–6 by E. T. Parris. These pictures are best viewed from the Whispering Gallery. Above the inner dome are the Stone Gallery and, highest of all at the base of the lantern, the Golden Gallery, both being exterior galleries.

The pavement under the dome is decorated with a huge compass design and carries the Latin epitaph for Wren, the composition of which is sometimes attributed to a later Surveyor, Robert Mylne. It may be translated as:

Beneath lies buried the founder of this church and city, Christopher Wren, who lived more than ninety years not for himself but for the public good. Reader, if you seek his monument, look around you.

The south-east quarter dome, depicting the Resurrection, can be seen in the photograph of the pulpit on page 45. The arms of the Goldsmiths' Company, which paid for it, can be seen below the mosaic surrounded by decorative stone carving. The other quarter domes were decorated at the expense of the following companies: north-east, the Merchant Taylors', north-west, the Mercers', and south-west, the Grocers'.

The pavement in the dome area with the compass design and Wren's epitaph. Note the heat-transfer grille.

Also in the pavement, a short distance from the choir steps, is the Churchill memorial. This is a simple statement, sculpted in bronze by John Skelton, which reads: 'The catafalque of Sir Winston Churchill stood here at his State funeral on 30th January 1965.'

To the left in front of the choir is the brass eagle lectern on a pedestal supported by four lions. It was made in 1719 by a founder named Jacob Sutton. On the opposite side is the pulpit, the fourth one to stand in the cathedral since the building was completed in 1710. The first was destroyed; the second one, built by Robert Mylne in 1803 is on the north triforium aisle and the third one may be seen in the crypt. This present one dates from 1964.

To mark the 250th anniversary of the completion of the cathedral Lord Mottistone, the then Surveyor to the Fabric, was commissioned by the Friends of St Paul's in the late 1950s to design a new pulpit and his drawing of it was exhibited at the Royal Academy in 1960. The working drawings were approved by Mottistone before his death in January 1963 and the pulpit was dedicated by the Bishop of London at the festival service of the Friends on 11 June 1964. The crucifix, which was carved by Edwin Russell, is a memorial to Lord Mottistone. The canopy was the gift of the Chapel Committee of the Order of the British Empire and the star of the Order can be seen on the undersurface.

The pulpit designed by Lord Mottistone, dedicated in 1964. The south-east quarter dome is to the right, above it.

The part of the organ on the north side with carvings by Grinling Gibbons (left).

On the north and south walls at the entrance to the CHOIR are the two parts of the organ. The original organ was built by Bernard Smith in 1697. Its case was made by Charles Hopson from Wren's design and the carvings were by Grinling Gibbons. The organ, with identical east and west fronts, was erected on a screen which shut off the choir area from the rest of the cathedral. Both Handel and Mendelssohn played on it when it was in that position.

John Seeley, later Lord Mottistone, was in partnership with Paul Paget, who succeeded him as Surveyor to the Fabric in 1963. Together they restored a number of war-damaged City churches during the 1950s, including All Hallows-by-the-Tower and the City Temple. They also designed the new Chandlers' Hall, Gresham Street, in 1958. In 1929 John Seeley restored a seventeenth-century house in Cloth Fair, Smithfield, in which he lived and worked for a number of years. From 1949 until 1955 Paul Paget was a Common Councilman of the City Corporation.

The preachers at Sunday matins in St Paul's Cathedral are given a bottle of sherry by the City Corporation. They also receive a sum of money from the same source. This happy custom is said to have developed from the fact that the Lord Mayor used to entertain the Paul's Cross preachers to luncheon.

Nowadays the lists of preachers are sent to the Keeper of the Guildhall who supplies the cheques and the wine. Until the outbreak of the Second World War the Keeper also sent with the year's supply of sherry, two bottles of brandy 'for cases of necessity'.

Number 41 Cloth Fair, restored by John Seeley, photographed from the churchyard of St Bartholomew-the-Great (right).

Henry Willis rebuilt the organ in 1872 and it was divided as it is now except that the console was originally at the north side. Additions and alterations to the instrument were made during the years 1897 to 1909 and again in 1930. It was stored in the crypt after the bombing of the chancel in October 1940 and suffered further damage when the north transept was hit during the air-raid of April 1941.

After further repairs and alteration in the late 1940s and in 1960, a major reconstruction was decided upon in 1973. This was undertaken by Noel Mander and the work was completed in April 1977. At that time a diapason chorus of four stops was added in the west gallery to overcome the time lag between the choir area and the west end; and the trumpets over the west door were installed. These additional sections are played from the main console.

This east end is where the building of the cathedral was started and consequently it was finished long before the nave and other parts. The choir was opened for worship on 2 December 1697 with a service of thanksgiving for the Treaty of Ryswick which marked the end of conflict between Louis XIV of France and William III of England. Henry Compton, Bishop of London throughout the thirty-five years of building, preached a sermon on the text: 'I was glad when they said unto me: we will go into the House of the Lord.' His congregation included the Lord Mayor and aldermen.

The present arrangement of the stalls dates from 1870 with the Dean's stall first on the south side or decani, and the Archdeacon of London's stall

The middle saucer dome of the choir ceiling depicting sea creatures.

The Bishop's Throne and choir stalls with carvings by Grinling Gibbons.

opposite on the north side, or cantoris. Halfway down the south side is the informal stall of the Bishop of London with the Lord Mayor's stall opposite. The Bishop's throne is at the east end of the south side and is used on official occasions. Its Latin name is *cathedra*, from which we derive the word 'cathedral' meaning the principal church of a diocese where the bishop's throne is.

Other stalls are allocated to the Residentiary Canons and the Minor Canons of St Paul's; to the Suffragan Bishops and the Archdeacons of the diocese and the thirty Prebendaries of St Paul's. Over each of these last stalls appears the name of the estate or prebend which formerly supported the occupant. The Latin phrase under each place name is the opening of the particular section of the Psalter which that prebendary used to recite daily. This French custom was introduced, with the permission of Dean Wulman, by Bishop Maurice in the year 1090.

The choir and sanctuary area is brilliant with Richmond mosaics and surely justifies the efforts of successive Deans, from Milman to Gregory, to realize Wren's frustrated intention to decorate St Paul's with mosaics and paintings. Every available space here carries mosaic work, from the panels over the organ to the easternmost bay; and the subjects range from Adam and Eve in the Garden to angels carrying the sign of the Passion.

The saucer domes portray the creation of the beasts, fish and birds which are exhorted in the Benedicite to bless the Lord. The Latin text appears on the western faces of the arches ('*Benedicite omnia opera. . .*'). Again, some livery companies contributed towards the cost of this work and their coats of arms are in the shields around the western saucer dome: the Merchant Taylors', the Mercers', the Fishmongers' and the Goldsmiths' Companies.

The present HIGH ALTAR, with its massive baldacchino or canopy, was designed by Stephen Dykes Bower and Godfrey Allen. Consecrated in May 1958, it is a memorial to members of the Commonwealth forces who died during the two World Wars. The altar is of Italian marble and the baldacchino of English oak.

It replaced the altar and reredos designed by G. F. Bodley and T. Garner and erected in 1888. That was a huge construction of pink marble towering up to the clerestory with many brass figures attached and a central carved Crucifixion scene. This was the cause of legal action by some extreme Protestants who considered it a superstitious object, but the Dean and Chapter finally won and the reredos remained until the Second World War. The cross and candlesticks on the present High Altar are 2.8 metres (9 foot 3 inches) and 1.6 metres (5 foot 6 inches) high respectively. They are of gilt bronze and the cross has an enamelled base of silver. The stones at the centre are amethyst and polished rock crystal. These ornaments were presented to the cathedral by the Goldsmiths' Company in 1958. High over the top of the baldacchino can be seen the easternmost of all the mosaics: the figure of Christ Triumphant, with recording angels in the panels on the north and south sides.

The Crypt

We return to the door to the crypt which is at the eastern end of the south transept. Through the open door may be seen the arch over the entrance to the steps leading down to the crypt which was originally a burial place, as the group of three death's-heads on the arch testifies. This *memento mori* was carved by William Kempster.

The CRYPT, or basement area, of St Paul's is remarkable in that it is as extensive as the cathedral ground floor instead of being confined to the east end of the building. It is not only the largest crypt in Europe but also one of the most impressive, because of the splendid vaulting designed by Wren.

In the latter part of the nineteenth century the crypt was completely restored. The thorough cleaning produced some 50 tonnes of plaster-dust, soot and dirt from the walls and windowsills. The broad wooden window sashes were replaced by narrow iron sashes, the roof was cleaned and painted and the floor relaid.

During the Second World War the St Paul's Watch control and communications centre was in the crypt and it was here, during many months of nightly bombing raids on the City, that the Dean and Chapter slept with their families.

Speaking in 1946, Godfrey Allen, the Surveyor to the Fabric, mentioned some of the wartime defence measures which he had carried out:

> Many of the famous monuments were encased in brickwork. A number of busts and statues were moved to safety and the well-known effigy of a former Dean, Dr Donne, which survived the fire of 1666, was transferred to the crypt where, during the desperate nights of 1940–41, it lay side by side with the present Dean when he was 'off-duty'.

From 16 November 1940 until 1 April 1945 all cathedral services were held down in the crypt. Among the more significant ones which took place were the memorial service for Pilot Officer William Fiske III, RAF (1911–40), the first American killed on active service during the Second World War; the Festival of the Sons of the Clergy service on 12 May 1941, which was conducted by the light of candles and oil lamps because of the destruction of all mains services by bombing; and, on appropriate dates each year, services for the Czech, Polish and Norwegian National Days.

There are many graves and tombs in the crypt, although burials no longer take place. In fact the last burial here was that of Admiral Beatty in March 1936, although the ashes of some cremated notables are laid here from time to time. There are also some 200 memorials, with more being added, so there is much to see.

The main items of interest are: the Chapel of the Order of the British Empire, the Wellington and Nelson tombs, the Treasury, the Great Model and the Lecture Room. Moving from east to west we shall look at

Cakes and ale in Stationers' Hall, Ash Wednesday 1935.

these in turn also mentioning some of the nearby graves, tombs and memorials.

The Most Excellent Order of the British Empire was founded by King George V in 1917 to honour all those who had rendered distinguished service to Britain. In 1957 it was decided that St Paul's Cathedral should be the church of the Order and that a CHAPEL OF THE ORDER OF THE BRITISH EMPIRE should be constructed. The site chosen was the area at the eastern end of the crypt known as the Chapel of St Faith which already housed an altar and other fittings.

The Church of St Faith which stood close by Old St Paul's was demolished in the thirteenth century to enable the east end of the cathedral to be enlarged. In return the parishioners of St Faith's were provided with a chapel in the crypt and, after the Great Fire, similar provision was made in Wren's building. Until 1878 the north aisle of the east end of the crypt belonged to St Faith's parishioners, many of whom were publishers and booksellers living and carrying on their business in the St Paul's Churchyard and Paternoster Row area.

The Chapel of St Faith is traditionally the chapel of the Stationers' Company and annually, on Ash Wednesday, the Master and Wardens lead a procession of members of the Company to a service in the chapel.

John Norton (d.1612), printer and bookseller, had a shop in St Paul's Churchyard known as the Queen's Head. Three times Master of the Stationers' Company, he was also an alderman of the City of London. He is buried in St Faith's Chapel in the crypt of Old St Paul's. One of John Norton's bequests was for the provision of cakes and ale for members of the Company on Ash Wednesdays and the custom is still maintained today.

Both the new chapel and its furnishings were designed by the Surveyor to the Fabric, Lord Mottistone, who declared at the outset that the existing Wren stonework, and particularly the vaulted ceiling, should be the major architectural feature of the chapel. With this in mind he made light and translucent enclosures consisting of wrought-iron grilles and glass panels.

The wrought-iron work was designed in the manner of Jean Tijou and made from Lord Mottistone's drawings by William Norris at his Brentford forge. The sixteen glass panels were painted in grisaille by Brian Thomas, who also designed the stained glass windows.

The first four panels carry portraits of the royal founders, King George V and Queen Mary, and of King George VI and Queen Elizabeth (now The Queen Mother); and HM The Queen and Prince Philip. The six panels on the north side of the chapel depict the various regions of the world, indicating the international nature of the Order. On the south-side panels the different forms of service to Britain for which appointments to the Order are made are illustrated. These range from professions such as the church, law, medicine and the armed forces, to communications, fine arts and sports.

The altar, made of Portland stone, is covered with a red velvet cloth which is embroidered in gold and silver silk with the star of a Knight Grand Cross of the Order. The altar cross and candlesticks are of wrought iron and bronze. The furniture and the font are of silvered wood and the upholstery is brocade in the colours of the Order – pink and pearl grey.

The EAST END of the crypt is a rich confusion of graves and memorials dating from within a few years of the start of Wren's building operations to the present day. Some of the earliest ones, which may be seen on the north side, are those of the parishioners of St Faith's.

First, we shall look at some of the more important and interesting memorials and graves in the south aisle of this chapel area. At the easternmost end are two attractive monuments facing each other. On the left, the memorial to Randolph Caldecott (1846–86) is a statuette of a little girl holding a medallion portrait of him. Born in England, this artist and book illustrator, most famous for his *John Gilpin* and other books for children, died in Florida. Since 1938 the Caldecott Medal has been awarded annually in the USA in his memory for the best illustrations in children's books.

The memorial to Wren's daughter Jane (1677–1702) is on the right. The white marble monument by Francis Bird shows a young lady seated at an organ to commemorate Jane Wren's musical talent. Nearby are memorials to other members of the Wren family including Susan Holder (1627–88), Sir Christopher's sister; and Constantia (1758–1851), his long-lived great-granddaughter.

On the left, below the first window recess, is the grave of Sir Christopher Wren himself (1632–1723) covered with a black marble slab. The inscription reads:

Here lieth
Sir Christopher Wren Kt
The Builder of this Cathedral
Church of St Paul &c
Who Dyed
in the Year of our Lord
MDCCXXIII
And of his Age XCI

The OBE Chapel, which is also the Chapel of St Faith. Mottistone's design emphasizes Wren's lovely vaulting.

John Rennie built Southwark Bridge (1815–19). It was later replaced by Sir Ernest George's construction in 1921. The present London Bridge, which was opened in 1973, superseded the one designed by Rennie and built from his plans by his son Sir John between the years 1825 and 1831. Rennie's London Bridge was bought and transported to America. It has now been re-erected at Lake Havasu, Arizona.

Until Robert Mylne's Blackfriars Bridge was erected in 1769, London Bridge was the only City bridge across the Thames. In 1869 its replacement, designed by Sir Joseph Cubitt, was opened by Queen Victoria.

The City Corporation maintains and, when necessary, replaces four bridges over the Thames: London Bridge, Southwark and Blackfriars Bridges and, although it is outside the City boundary, Tower Bridge.

John Rennie's Southwark Bridge, which survived for over 100 years, was replaced in 1921.

On the wall above the grave is a plaque bearing the Latin epitaph which we have already seen under the dome on the cathedral floor, ending: '. . . *Lector, si monumentum requiris, circumspice*'. Below this a more simply worded memorial to the stonemason brothers involved in the building of the cathedral, Edward and Thomas Strong, is no less eloquent: 'Remember the men who made shapely the stones of St Paul's Cathedral 1675–1708.' This tablet was erected by the Masons' Company in 1975 to mark the tercentenary of the laying of the foundation stone.

In the next window recess is the memorial to Bishop Reginald Heber (1783–1826), the hymn writer who was Bishop of Calcutta from 1823 until his death at Trichinopoly. The kneeling figure of Heber was sculpted by Francis Chantrey and is the last of three monuments to the Bishop which he executed.

Beneath the Heber memorial lies the tomb of John Rennie (1761–1821), the Scottish civil engineer who settled in London in 1784. He was famous for his construction of canals, docks and, particularly, bridges.

From left to right:
The large bronze crucifix, executed by the American artist John Singer Sargent (1856–1925) himself, is now his memorial.

The Blake memorial tablet, sculpted in 1927 by Henry Poole.

Ernest Gillick's memorial to George Frampton (1860–1928) includes a small replica of Frampton's Peter Pan statue in Kensington Gardens.

Blackfriars Bridge, built by Robert Mylne in 1769, was the second City bridge across the Thames.

This chapel area is often called Painters' Corner or, more aptly, Artists' Corner because there are, in addition to painters, many sculptors buried or commemorated here. Some of the more important ones are: Lawrence Alma-Tadema (1836–1912), John Constable (1776–1837), Joseph Edgar Boehm (1834–90), Henry Fuseli (1741–1825), William Holman Hunt (1827–1910), Edwin Landseer (1802–73), Thomas Lawrence (1769–1830), Frederic Leighton (1830–96), John Everett Millais (1829–96) and Joshua Reynolds (1723–92). Some of the more recent memorials include: Muirhead Bone (1876–1953), W. Reid Dick (1879–1961), Alfred Gilbert (1854–1934), Alfred Munnings (1878–1959), Edward Poynter (1836–1919), Wilson Steer (1860–1942), W. Hamo Thornycroft (1850–1925) and Charles Wheeler (1892–1974).

The busts of Dean William Ralph Inge by Henry Pegram, and Canon Sidney Arthur Alexander by W. Reid Dick, in the Library.

Also in this area are the grave and memorial of the architect and engineer Robert Mylne (1734–1811) who was Surveyor to the Fabric of St Paul's from 1766 to 1811; and of the architects George Dance the Younger (1741–1825), Edwin Lutyens (1869–1944) and Albert Richardson (1880–1964).

In the middle aisle are the graves of Deans Gregory (1819–1911) and Milman (1791–1868) and of Canon Alexander (1866–1948); while further to the north there are memorial tablets on the wall to Deans Inge (1860–1954), Matthews (1881–1973) and Sullivan (1910–80). Over in the easternmost window niche of the north aisle is the effigy of Canon Liddon (1829–90).

In the north-east corner there is St Christopher's Chapel. This is the children's chapel and many visiting parties use it. A stained glass panel above the altar depicts St Christopher carrying the Christ child.

Some other churchmen commemorated in this area are Canon Newbolt (1844–1930), Archdeacon Hale (1795–1870), Canon Scott Holland (1847–1918) and John Jackson (1811–85) who was Bishop of London from 1869 to 1885.

Canon Sidney Arthur Alexander was Treasurer of St Paul's from 1909 to 1948 and Chapter Treasurer for most of that time. He was therefore responsible for the fabric and the finances of the cathedral for almost forty years.

His scheme for the preservation of St Paul's, which he launched in 1913, was completed in 1930 and in three public appeals he raised £400,000. Much of the money was given by City institutions and individuals.

At the same time, however, Canon Alexander was forced to do battle with the City Corporation over a number of issues in addition to the Dangerous Structure controversy already mentioned. The most serious and longest running disagreement was that con-

cerning St Paul's Bridge.

In 1911 the Corporation introduced a Bill in Parliament which was passed and became the Corporation of London (Bridges) Act 1911. This enabled the City to erect a new Blackfriars Bridge and an additional bridge between Southwark and Blackfriars Bridges which was named the St Paul's Bridge. The resulting traffic on the north bank would pass on a new road to be constructed within 9 metres (30 feet) of the eastern end of the cathedral.

Canon Alexander fought the plan then and when it was revived after completion of the new Blackfriars Bridge in 1921. He believed that the proposed bridge and the consequent

increase in north–south traffic posed a serious threat to the fabric of St Paul's and would interfere with access to the building and the conduct of services.

He gained the support of many influential people and by 1929 the St Paul's Bridge plan was abandoned.

Following this success Canon Alexander was engaged from 1930 to 1935 on his plan to protect the cathedral foundations by a 'sacred area' around the building within which no excavation would be permitted. The City authorities gave him their support and a Bill to this end was introduced in Parliament by the Corporation which became law in June 1935.

Among the journalists commemorated in this area of the crypt are W. H. Russell (1820–1907), the famous war correspondent of *The Times* who exposed the appalling mismanagement of the Crimean War; Archibald Forbes (1838–1900) of the *Daily News* and Melton Prior (1845–1910), who was also an artist and worked for the *Illustrated London News* for thirty years. Another memorial commemorates the special correspondents who were killed while reporting the campaigns in the Sudan from 1883 to 1885, including those who wrote for all of the following: *The Times, Morning Post, Standard, Daily News, Manchester Guardian* and Reuters.

There are tablets and other memorials to many of the organist-composers of St Paul's, including Handel's friend Maurice Greene (1695?–1755), who was also Professor of Music at Cambridge. Greene was first buried in St Olave Jewry but when the church was demolished in 1888 his remains were removed to the tomb of the composer William Boyce (1710–79) here in the crypt. Thomas Attwood (1765–1838), a pupil of Mozart, is buried here and there is a memorial to his successor John Goss (1800–80). The tomb of George C. Martin (1844–1916) is to the north-east of Goss while his memorial, by Henry Pegram, is to the north-west. Charles Macpherson (1870–1927), his wife Sophie and his son Alasdair are buried together next to the man who succeeded him as organist, Stanley Marchant (1883–1949).

A plan showing the proposed St Paul's Bridge and road past the east end of the cathedral.

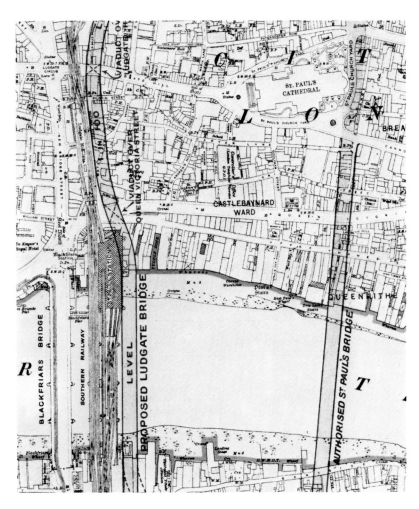

Moving out of the chapel, on the left there is a memorial plaque, with a bas-relief profile, to the composer and writer of musicals, Ivor Novello (1893–1951) and, on the right, the memorial bust by Jacob Epstein of the Labour politician, Sir Stafford Cripps (1889–1952). We now go down a couple of steps to the next area in the middle of which stands the WELLINGTON TOMB.

This massive construction was not completed until six years after Wellington's death. It was designed by Francis Penrose, Surveyor to the Fabric, from a preliminary sketch made in 1852 by his predecessor C. R. Cockerell. The sarcophagus, consisting of two large blocks of Cornish porphyry, is set on a plinth of granite with a lion's head sculpted at each corner. The mosaic floor in this part of the crypt was made during the 1850s by women prisoners at Woking jail.

On the walls of the Wellington tomb area are ten memorial tablets to the Field Marshals who were leaders of the military forces of the British Commonwealth during the Second World War and to those who served under them. The memorials were dedicated on 23 November 1979 in the presence of HM Queen Elizabeth II by the then Archbishop of Canterbury, Dr Donald Coggan.

The Wellington tomb with Nelson's tomb beyond.

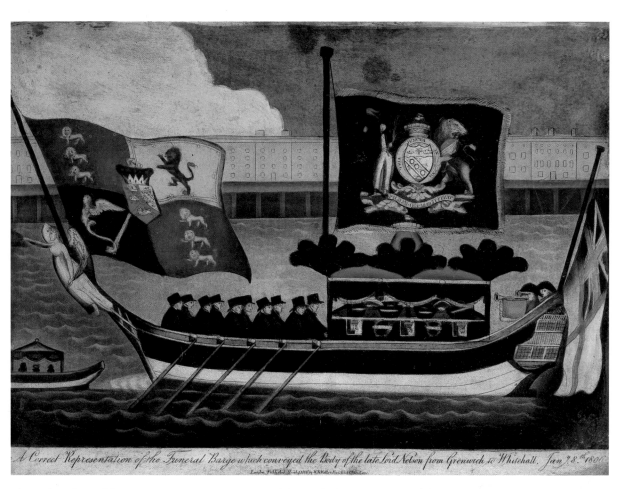

A Correct Representation of the Funeral Barge which conveyed the Body of the late Lord Nelson from Grenwich to Whitehall. Jan 8.th 1806

London. Published March 12 1806 by W.Walker Cornhill & Cheapside.

The Nelson funeral barge passing through the City on its way to Westminster. A painting on glass in the Library.

The Field Marshals commemorated are: Viscount Alanbrooke (1883–1963), Earl Alexander (1891–1969), Sir Claude Auchinleck (1884–1981), Sir John Dill (1881–1944), Viscount Gort (1886–1946), Baron Ironside (1880–1959), Viscount Montgomery (1887–1976), Viscount Slim (1891–1970), Earl Wavell (1883–1950) and Baron Wilson (1881–1964).

Passing through to the Nelson tomb area we see on the left the memorial plaque to the men and women of the Air Transport Auxiliary who died ferrying aircraft to theatres of war during the years 1939–45. Beneath the plaque there is a Roll of Honour in a glass-topped case. Nearby is the memorial to Florence Nightingale (1820–1910), the hospital reformer and founder of modern nursing.

The NELSON TOMB, sited within a beautiful octagon of pillars and vaulting directly under the dome area, comprises a black marble sarcophagus on a granite base. The sarcophagus was originally part of an elaborate design created by Benedetto da Rovezzano for Cardinal Wolsey for his own tomb. With Wolsey's downfall, initially over the question of Henry VIII's divorce from Catherine of Aragon, the sarcophagus was seized for the King. It remained at Windsor until the reign of George III when it was decided to use it as a tomb for Nelson.

Nelson's coffin was made from the mainmast of the French flagship *L'Orient*, destroyed during the Battle of the Nile. The mosaic floor has anchors and other nautical emblems worked in it together with Nelson's famous signal to the fleet before the Battle of Trafalgar: 'England expects every man to do his duty.'

Nelson's great contemporary, Admiral Collingwood (1750–1810), is buried nearby. He entered the navy aged 11, played a prominent part in several famous victories, including Trafalgar, and died at sea at the age of 60.

Another Trafalgar hero, Admiral Carnegie, Earl of Northesk (1758–1831), is buried just to the north of Nelson. The tombs of the two foremost British naval leaders during the First World War – Admirals Jellicoe (1859–1935) and Beatty (1871–1936) – lie side by side in the south-east recess. Beatty, although unwell, attended Jellicoe's funeral and died four months later. His was the last body to be buried in St Paul's.

The TREASURY of the Diocese of London is to the north of these naval tombs and is reached by turning right. The carpeted area, which forms an approach to the Treasury proper, has a number of interesting exhibits. At the entrance, on the left, is a copy of the bust of Sir Christopher Wren by Edward Pierce, the original of which is in the Ashmolean Museum at Oxford, and his death mask. Wren's penknife, measuring rod and other implements are also in this case. On the opposite side is the effigy of Sir William Cokain, or Cokayne (d.1626) from Old St Paul's. Cokain was Lord Mayor from 1619 to 1620. His funeral sermon which was preached by the Dean, John Donne, contained this often-quoted passage:

> I throw myself down in my chamber, and I call in, and invite God,
> and his Angels thither, and when they are there, I neglect God
> and his Angels, for the noise of a fly, for the rattling of a coach,
> for the whining of a door.

There are several models of parts of Wren's cathedral on display and a model of Old St Paul's. On the left, among a number of artefacts, is a skeleton key which was found on the floor of the strongroom after the robbery of 21 or 22 December 1810. The whole of the cathedral plate and the solid silver covers of a Common Prayer and of Bishop Compton's folio Bible were stolen.

Opposite the entrance gates to the Treasury itself is the damaged effigy from Old St Paul's of Sir Nicholas Bacon (1509–79), the father of Sir Francis Bacon.

The decorative and functional steel entry gates to the Treasury were the subject of a design competition, organized by the Crafts Council, which was won by Alan Evans. Beyond the gates are treasures of St Paul's Cathedral as well as those from many of the parish churches throughout the diocese. Most of the cathedral plate of Old St Paul's was confiscated on the order of Henry VIII and the remainder was taken in 1553, the last year of Edward VI's reign. The richly embroidered and bejewelled vestments and altar cloths were removed at the same time.

Again, the precious metal vessels and ornaments which were acquired over the next ninety years were confiscated and sold by order of Parliament in April 1644. As the *House of Lords Calendar* tells us, the money resulting from the sale was to be 'employed towards the providing of necessaries for the Train of Artillery by the Committee at Grocers' Hall'.

The silver plate given to mark the Restoration of the monarchy in 1660 and other items subsequently acquired were all taken in the robbery of 1810. Since then a copper-gilt set of vessels has been purchased and some pieces of silver plate have been donated. In 1872 a handsome silver gilt alms dish, presented to the cathedral the previous year, was lent to the Guildhall Library for inclusion in the exhibition marking its official opening to the public. In addition to the liturgical plate on display are several secular items including wine cups, tobacco jars and silver-topped staves.

The Jubilee cope seen through the closed Treasury gates.

Some of the sets of vestments and altar frontals acquired by the cathedral since their restoration into Anglican worship in 1897 are exhibited here, including the cope given to Bishop Mandell Creighton by his friend Offley Wakeman. It was made from the cloth woven for the coronation dress of the Empress Frederick of Germany (Queen Victoria's eldest child, Victoria), but her husband died before he could be crowned and the dress was not made.

In a letter dated 19 February 1904 to Mrs Creighton (which is held in the library) Mrs Wakeman explained all this and then added: 'I think I am right in saying that it is not *part* of what was woven but the whole of it and is, therefore, the only piece of brocade with that special historical interest.'

Also on display is the Jubilee Cope (1977) which was designed by Beryl Dean and embroidered by students of the Stanhope Institute under her direction.

Two of the cathedral manuscripts exhibited here are a charter granted by Richard II to the College of Minor Canons of St Paul's in 1394 and Avicenna's *Canones Medicinae*, presented to the cathedral in 1451. Avicenna (980–1037) was a Persian described as 'the prince of physicians'.

In the fourteenth century the Goldsmiths' Company undertook to maintain a chantry in the chapel of its patron saint – St Dunstan's Chapel in St Paul's Cathedral. In succeeding centuries the Goldsmiths have had close links with, and have been generous in their gifts to, St Paul's.

On many occasions significant sums of money have been given towards programmes of major repairs to the cathedral. Specific gifts have included, as we have seen, the mosaic over the pulpit and the gilt cross and candlesticks on the High Altar. Contributions have also been made towards the cost of the present gold communion plate, designed in 1934 by Sir Edwin Lutyens, and the setting up of the Diocesan Treasury.

Staff of the Museum of London, which is in the City's Barbican development, assisted in the setting-up of the Treasury displays and Charles Oman, the authority on English church plate, gave invaluable advice. Oman died in 1982 – the year after the Treasury was opened – and he is commemorated by a plaque in the crypt.

There are several graves and memorials in the public part of the aisle running from north to south. Starting at the entrance to the Treasury area there is a monument on the left to R. J. Seddon (1845–1906), Prime Minister of New Zealand, sculpted by George Frampton; immediately behind this is the bronze head of T. E. Lawrence (1888–1935) – Lawrence of Arabia – by Eric Kennington.

Opposite Seddon on the right is a group of memorials to other New Zealand and Australian statesmen: William Bede Dalley (1831–88), W. M. Hughes (1864–1952) and Sir George Grey (1812–98). Below the Grey memorial is the grave of Sir Charles Bradley Pritchard (1837–1903), the colonial administrator in India.

Next on the left is the bust of George Washington (1732–99). This is one of three busts of Washington sent to Britain in 1921 by President Warren Harding on behalf of the American people. The other two were for Liverpool City Hall and Sulgrave Manor, the sixteenth-century ancestral home of the Washington family in Northamptonshire. In his message accompanying the busts the President expressed the hope that they would remind people both of the common sacrifice of the American and British nations during the First World War and of the fact that Washington was 'an Englishman by birth and tradition'.

On the same side there is a memorial to the colonial administrator Sir Henry Bartle Frere (1815–84) and also a plaque commemorating William Ewert Berry, Viscount Camrose (1879–1954), the newspaper proprietor. The latter was unveiled by Sir Winston Churchill in 1956. Next is the grave of George Cruikshank (1792–1878) the notable caricaturist and book illustrator and, further down on the right-hand side, there is a memorial tablet to him.

After working as a reporter on various newspapers in South Wales, William Ewert Berry came to London in 1898 and soon founded *Advertising World*. His brother Gomer joined him and their fortunes were based on the paper's success. In 1915 they bought the *Sunday Times* where William was the editor-in-chief for twenty-one years.

The brothers then formed Allied Newspapers with E. M. Iliffe in 1924 and by 1928 the group controlled three national daily newspapers – the *Daily Telegraph*, *Daily Dispatch* and the *Financial Times* – fourteen provincial dailies, eight provincial weekly newspapers and seventy periodicals.

The Daily Telegraph *building in 1938 when William Ewert Berry was Editor-in-Chief.*

After this there is a bas-relief bust of Edward Vansittart Neale (1810–92), the pioneer Christian Socialist; and next, a memorial tablet to the St John's Ambulance men who died in the Boer War, 1899–1902. On the other side is the only piece of sculpture in St Paul's by the French sculptor Auguste Rodin – the bust of the English poet and critic, W. E. Henley (1849–1903). The monument on the right to Sir William Huggins (1824–1910) the astronomer, which has a bas-relief bust of him and a cameo of his wife Margaret, was sculpted by Henry Pegram.

Finally on the right, a tablet commemorates Pilot Officer William Fiske III (see page 52). Fiske was severely wounded in aerial combat during the Battle of Britain and died two days later in hospital in Chichester, West Sussex. Under his name the inscription reads: 'An American citizen, who died that England might live.'

Opposite the Fiske memorial is an entrance to part of the south aisle where some of the effigies from Old St Paul's which survived the Great Fire – although blackened and damaged – may be seen. There are also two of the original 'incense potts' from the south portico which were carved by Caius Gabriel Cibber.

Some larger than life-size statues, formerly in the north transept on the cathedral floor, are now here: General Sir Charles Napier (1782–1853) and his brother, General Sir William Napier (1785–1860); and Admirals Sir Pulteney Malcolm (1768–1838) and Lord Rodney (1719–92).

At the far end is the marble effigy of Henry Hart Milman (1791–1868), the work of Francis Williamson. Milman, a poet and historian, was Dean of St Paul's from 1849 to 1868.

Approaching the Great Model we pass several memorials of interest. On the left is a tablet, with a profile, to the novelist Charles Reade (1814–84) and a bust of the writer Walter Besant (1836–1901) who was a founder member of the Society of Authors. The next three plaques commemorate George Smith (1824–1901) who published works by Charlotte Brontë, Ruskin and Thackeray and who founded the *Dictionary of National Biography*; W. G. Holford (1907–75) the architect who was the consultant for the rebuilding of the City of London after the Second World War; and the Reverend Richard Harris Barham (1788–1845) who is discussed on page 84. Last on this side is the memorial, with profile, to the founder of the Church Army, the Reverend Wilson Carlile (1847–1942). On the right-hand side is a large memorial by Onslow Ford to George Swan Nottage (1822–85), one of only two Lord Mayors of London to have died in office; the other one was William Beckford (1709–70).

The plaque to Baron Thomson of Fleet (1894–1976) describes the Canadian-born newspaper proprietor as: 'A strange and adventurous man from nowhere, ennobled by the great virtues of courage and integrity and faithfulness.'

The Conservative politician, minister and diplomat Alfred Duff Cooper, 1st Viscount Norwich (1890–1954), is commemorated simply as: 'Duff Cooper, Statesman and Writer'.

Finally there is the memorial by George Frampton to George Williams (1821–1905), the founder of the Young Men's Christian Association. It consists of a bust of Williams with two supporting female figures.

Continuing further westwards we now come to the GREAT MODEL itself. This was the second model for the new St Paul's made for Christopher Wren. It was constructed from Wren's drawings traced on to oak boards by the master joiner William Cleere and and twelve assistants, during the years 1673–4. The softwood decorative carving was done by Richard Cleere.

The Great Model, which was constructed in 1673–4 from Wren's favourite design, is now refurbished and sited in the crypt.

Over three centuries this Great Model has been alternately cherished and neglected. Until 1858 it was kept in what is now known as the 'Trophy Room' on the north aisle of the triforium but which was then called the 'Model Room'. It was then removed to the South Kensington Museum (the forerunner of the Science and the Natural History Museums) where, after being refurbished, it remained on exhibition until 1873. After that date it was returned to the cathedral and was deposited at the western end of the triforium north aisle. 'It is', wrote J. S Bumpus in 1913, 'in a shamefully dirty and mutilated state, and has suffered considerably from removal . . . steps should be taken to restore this precious relic.' In 1929 the model was repaired and re-sited in the Trophy Room where it was viewable by appointment.

In 1982, to commemorate the 350th anniversary of Wren's birth, it was again extensively refurbished and placed here in the crypt. The surrounding series of frames of historical notes, plans and photographs was devised and organized by the Wren scholar, Professor Kerry Downes. This display of the Great Model and the related material was unveiled by Queen Elizabeth The Queen Mother on 1 July 1982.

67

H. Pilkington's picture (above) shows part of the road, St Paul's Churchyard, and the south-west aspect of the cathedral as they might have been in the 1930s if Wren had been allowed to build from his favourite design. The picture belongs to the Dean and Chapter of St Paul's.

Beyond the Great Model is the octagonal VICTORIAN PULPIT constructed in various types of marble in 1861 from a design by Francis Penrose. It is a memorial to Captain Robert Fitzgerald (1817–53) of the Punjab Frontier Force Cavalry and was the cathedral pulpit for over 100 years. It was replaced by the present pulpit after the Watch Night Service on 31 December 1963. A framed enlargement of a photograph taken before the Second World War shows the marble pulpit in place under the dome on the cathedral floor. The Victorian marble reredos and High Altar, with which the pulpit was in keeping, are also to be seen in the picture.

On the opposite side of the aisle is the LECTURE ROOM of the cathedral which was opened by Queen Elizabeth The Queen Mother on 28 June 1983. Here, at frequent intervals throughout the day, programmes of colour slides with spoken commentary illustrating the history, architecture and decoration of St Paul's are presented.

Continuing to the west end of the crypt, the monument to General Sir William Ponsonby (1772–1815) by E. H. Baily is on the left. The memorial states that the General 'fell gloriously at the Battle of Waterloo on 18th June 1815'. Wellington, in his report of the battle, described Ponsonby as 'an ornament to his profession'.

On the wall on the right a tablet lists the Deans' Virgers and the Clerks of the Works since 1663. Nearby, another tablet is 'In pious memory of the famous dead whose remains lay buried in Old St Paul's Cathedral or whose memorials perished in its destruction.' The chronological list which follows is headed by Sebba, King of the East Saxons (d.677), and ends with Bryan Walton, a prebendary of St Paul's and later, Bishop of Chester (d.1661), who edited a Polyglot Bible which was printed in 1657. The cathedral Library possesses a very rare large paper edition of this Bible.

In 1628 Bryan Walton was presented to the living of St Martin Orgar, Cannon Street. He quickly took up the cause of the City clergy in their struggle to obtain the tithe due to them on rents. There was at that time widespread evasion of full payment and Walton calculated that all the City aldermen and the 200 Common Councilmen paid less on their properties than did 'six farmers in the country'.

As the law then stood actions for non payment of tithe were heard before the Lord Mayor! An appeal by the clergy to Charles I in 1634 led to the forming of a committee to consider the problem but its meetings proved inconclusive. However, in 1638 the clergy were given leave to sue for non payment of tithe in the ecclesiastical courts.

The portrait of Bryan Walton by Pierre Lombart which appears as the frontispiece to the Biblia Polyglotta.

The Cathedral Environs

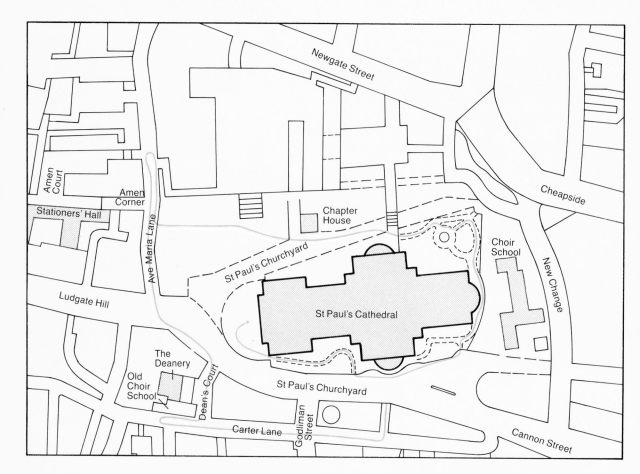

A plan of the environs showing the direction of the tour.

or the starting point of our tour of the environs we return to the FORECOURT at the west end of the cathedral. The forecourt, which is a popular gathering place for tourists, sightseers and others, was first completely opened to the public just over 100 years ago. It was in January 1874 that the original iron railings enclosing the west end of the cathedral were sold at auction and raised a total of £349. Some of the railings went to form an entrance gate to Lewes Castle in East Sussex. Another section was shipped over to Canada where it was used to surround the tomb of J. G. Harper and his wife in High Park, Toronto.

The west end forecourt before the railings were removed in 1874.

Here, at the bottom of the steps at the west end of St Paul's, Queen Victoria arrived on Tuesday, 22 June 1897, during her royal progress through London. She had come to give thanks to God for the sixty years of her reign. The 78-year-old Queen stayed in her carriage and a short service was held on the steps.

The Dean and Chapter wore magnificent copes and red velvet skull-caps. It was the first time cathedral clergy had worn such splendid garb since the seventeenth century. The Lambeth Conference – the conference of bishops from the whole Anglican Communion – was being held at the same time and as a result over 100 bishops attended the thanksgiving service.

Queen Victoria's Diamond Jubilee year visit to St Paul's Cathedral is commemorated in a Memorial Paving Stone in the forecourt, at the bottom of the steps and in line with the Great West Door.

An artist's impression of the New Year's Eve crowd at the west end of St Paul's in 1897.

The royal procession nearing London Bridge from King William Street, 1897, to celebrate Queen Victoria's Diamond Jubilee.

From the time the forecourt was fully opened to the public, large noisy crowds gathered there to greet the New Year. On 31 December 1934, the year of his appointment as Dean of St Paul's, Dr Matthews decided to hold a Watch Night Service inside the cathedral while outside, Canon Dick Sheppard, accompanied by a Salvation Army band, was to address the crowd from the top of the steps.

The service inside the cathedral was a great success and Watch Night Services have been held at St Paul's ever since. Outside, however, the less sober individuals heckled Canon Sheppard. 'He soon became', wrote Matthews in *A History of St Paul's Cathedral*, 'the target of empty whisky bottles.' As a result, the City police 'refused to allow any further open-air evangelistic efforts on New Year's Eve'.

The rowdy crowd transferred its allegiance to the West End of London, particularly Trafalgar Square, shortly after the end of the Second World War.

The description in the *City Press* (23 June 1897) of Queen Victoria's progress through the Square Mile was effusive:

Punctuality is the courtesy of kings, and the Queen, as is her habit, was punctual. The Colonial procession, headed by the band of the Royal Horse Guards, passed along the first half of the line of route a little before nine o'clock and took up their station in St Paul's Churchyard. Needless to say, they were enthusiastically cheered by the assembled multitudes. The Royal procession followed shortly after eleven. It was a magnificent and picturesque sight. The bright uniforms, the arms gleaming in the sunshine, the spirit-stirring strains of the martial music; the dark-visaged soldiers from Asia and Africa, representing and symbolising the world-wide Empire over which the Queen presides, raised to an almost uncontrollable pitch the enthusiasm of the myriad spectators, which found vent in long and loud cheers. And what a crowd it was! The Queen herself has never looked upon such a sight. We leave it to others to estimate the number of spectators, and content ourselves with saying, what it is perfectly safe to say, that so large a crowd has never before filled the City streets: and when at last the Royal State carriage with its cream-coloured horses and its venerable occupant accompanied by the Princess of Wales and the Princess Christian passed, the scene baffled description.

Just behind us, as we stand at the memorial paving stone, is the Statue of Queen Anne. The original statue was carved in 1712 from marble supplied by the Queen herself. The sculptor was Francis Bird whose other work, both outside and inside the cathedral, we have already seen. Queen Anne, in her robes of state, holds the orb and sceptre; the four female figures around the pedestal represent Britain, Ireland, France and North America.

From the time it was erected, Bird's statue caused much controversy, especially over the fact that the Queen has her back to the cathedral. The visual advantage of this particular siting, however, is that the face of the statue stands with the great west façade of St Paul's as a backdrop.

The statue was attacked in 1743 by a person described as 'a lunatic' and the Queen's nose was broken off. In 1768 the surrounding figures lost their noses and the Queen her orb and sceptre in a further 'lunatic attack'. The statue suffered increasing decay and frequent defacement over the next 100 years. On 6 February 1882 R. R. Green recorded in his diary: 'A lunatic, taken into custody for damaging the statue of Queen Anne, sent to an Asylum.' Two years after that incident Bird's Queen Anne was removed and it is now in the grounds of a girls' school in East Sussex.

Frederick Cleary with Dean Sullivan after the unveiling of Becket.

Other work by Christopher Kempster may be seen at St Mary Abchurch, Abchurch Lane. The carved cherubs over the windows and all the other outside stonework were done by him.

Continuing the tour of the environs in an anti-clockwise direction, we go from the Queen Anne statue to the south-west corner of the cathedral, passing through the gap in the low wall which, until recently, supported iron railings which have now been removed.

Immediately on our left is the DEAN'S DOORWAY, so called because it is the nearest door to the Old Deanery which stands in Dean's Court on the opposite side of the road. We shall be looking at the Old Deanery later. The stone carvings of cherub faces with falling tears and the decorations on the pediment above the door and on the capitals of the pilasters at the sides are probably by William Kempster who did much of the stonework in the south-west tower.

Next to the Dean's Doorway is the outside wall of the Chapel of St Michael and St George. As this chapel was originally the Consistory, the coat of arms and mitre of the then Bishop of London, Henry Compton, appear under the window. The carving was done by Jonathan Maine.

The panels beneath the other twenty-six windows, which we shall see as we go round, were all carved by Grinling Gibbons.

We can walk along this inside path towards the south portico. On the left-hand side of the path is the dramatic, falling figure, *Becket*. This bronze representation of Archbishop Thomas Becket at the moment of his murder in Canterbury Cathedral in 1170 is by Bainbridge Copnall.

Thomas Becket was born a short distance from St Paul's in Cheapside. Although he was a prebendary of St Paul's Cathedral *in absentia* his relationship with the City was stormy. In 1169, as Archbishop of Canterbury in exile in Soissons, he excommunicated the Dean of St Paul's, Hugh de Mareni, and the Bishop of London, Gilbert Foliot.

This statue of Becket was paid for by the City Corporation. The unveiling ceremony was performed in May 1973 by Frederick Cleary, Chairman of the Corporation's Trees, Gardens and City Open Spaces Committee.

As we reach the south transept and SOUTH PORTICO we must move out on to the pavement. This portico is seldom used as an entrance or exit and consequently it receives relatively little attention although it is well worth studying. The master masons responsible for this area were Christopher Kempster and Ephraim Beauchamp.

The statues on the top of the transept represent, from left to right, the apostles Simon, Thomas (the Doubter), Andrew, Bartholomew and Matthias (chosen by lot to succeed Judas Iscariot). The original carvings by Francis Bird had become dangerous through decay and in 1900 three of them were extensively restored. In 1923 the remaining two were replaced by copies.

Caius Gabriel Cibber carved the Phoenix, 6 metres long by 3 metres high (18 × 9 foot), in the pediment and the word 'Resurgam' (I shall rise

again) underneath it. The image of the phoenix represents the new cathedral rising from the ashes of the old one. The choice of the motto 'Resurgam' is explained in *Parentalia*, the book about the Wren family by Sir Christopher's son Christopher, thus:

> In the Beginning of the new Works of St Paul's an Incident was taken notice of by some People as a memorable Omen, when a common Labourer was ordered to bring a flat stone from the Heaps of Rubbish . . . to be laid for a Mark and Direction to the Masons, the Stone which was immediately brought and laid down for that Purpose happened to be a Piece of Grave-stone with nothing remaining of the Inscription but this single word in large capitals RESURGAM.

The south portico is currently being restored. One major part of the restoration is the carving of four replacement vases by the cathedral's carvers. The original vases or 'incense potts' as they were described in the cathedral Account Books, were the work of Caius Gabriel Cibber and two of them may be seen in the Crypt.

A little further along the pavement is a gate at the south-east corner of the railings. This is a good place from which to look up at the BALL AND CROSS which are some 110 metres (365 feet) above the ground, at the top of the dome. The original ball and cross were made in copper by Andrew Niblett in 1708 from designs by Francis Bird. The present replacements were designed and erected in 1821 by the Surveyor to the Fabric, C. R. Cockerell. There is a model in the library of the Cockerell ball and cross.

The 1971 appeal for funds for the restoration of the fabric of St Paul's was supported by the Lord Mayor, Sir Peter Studd, who made it the theme of his mayoral year. City organizations and companies responded with their customary generosity and, in addition, handsome donations were received from Commonwealth countries and from the USA.

Dean Martin Sullivan and Sir Peter Studd, the Lord Mayor, launching the 1971 St Paul's appeal on the roof.

We now come into ST PAUL'S OPEN SPACE. This area of well-tended lawns, flowerbeds, bushes and trees stretching around the south and east sides and part of the north side of the cathedral, was formerly the burial grounds of St Paul's and neighbouring churches.

Virger Green wrote in his diary: 'Monday 22nd September 1879, the churchyard opened to the public as a garden; the Lord Mayor and Sheriffs and Canon Stubbs met at the Chapter House at 2.30 p.m.' Some additional land was incorporated into the scheme in 1966 when the present Open Space was formed.

The whole area is maintained by gardeners employed by the City Corporation. From time to time additional trees and bushes are planted, with due ceremony, by the Lord Mayor or some other dignitary, to mark special anni-versaries and other occasions. There are many interesting plaques in the gardens such as the two in the south-east corner. The first marks the planting of a Sweet Gum tree by the Lord Mayor, Sir Murray Fox, on 20 June 1975 to commemorate the 300th anniversary of the laying of the cathedral foundation stone in 1675. The second one is in the rose garden, presented by the Royal National Rose Society and the Rose Growers' Association in 1976, where the Lord Mayor, Sir Lindsay Ring, planted a climbing rose named Handel.

People enjoying the quiet of the Jubilee Gardens Open Space (left).

Derek Sutton, Headmaster of the cathedral Choir School (below).

After a few paces we come to the EAST END of the cathedral. This is the part of the exterior which most critics find architecturally disappointing. None the less there is a fine stone carving by Grinling Gibbons beneath the windows. The initials of the monarchs reigning at the time the work was done – William III and Queen Mary – are carved here.

To the right is the cathedral CHOIR SCHOOL which stands beyond the railings in New Change. There the thirty-eight choristers of St Paul's are boarded and receive their musical and general education.

On Ascension Day, 4 May 1967, just one week before his retirement from St Paul's, Dean Matthews performed his last official function. He accompa-nied the Lord Mayor, Sir Robert Bellinger, to the new Choir School and handed him the key for the opening ceremony.

Just past the east end of the cathedral, a paving stone marks the site where PAUL'S CROSS stood for hundreds of years until the mid-seventeenth century. Paul's Cross was not only an open-air pulpit for the preaching of sermons, but also a general meeting place for the citizens where papal and royal edicts were delivered, political matters were discussed and some trials were held.

Many churchmen and lay people did penance at Paul's Cross for various offences ranging from slander and adultery to heresy and sedition. Penitent heretics were made to stand for the duration of a sermon, dressed in white sheets and holding a bundle of faggots and a taper, to remind them and the assembled crowd of the awful death by burning which awaited those who did not repent. From time to time the preacher would strike them with a rod.

The burning of the Protestant John Rogers for heresy during Queen Mary's reign.

Henry Machyn, a Merchant Taylor and funeral furnisher in the City of London, recorded in his diary (1550–63) many incidents which occurred at Paul's Cross. He frequently mentions the attendance of the Lord Mayor, as in the first year of Queen Mary's reign, 1553, for example:

The xx day of August did preach at Paul's Cross Master Watson, chaplain, and there were all the Crafts of London in their best livery . . . and my Lord Mayor and the Aldermen and 200 of the guard to see no disquiet done.

A week earlier Dr Bourne, Rector of High Ongar in Essex, had preached at the cross. According to Machyn there was 'great uproar and shouting at his sermon, hurly burly and throwing up of caps'. He then added, 'If the Lord Mayor had not been there, there would have been great mischief done.' The crowd was finally calmed down by two popular preachers, John Bradford and John Rogers.

The latter, who was vicar of St Sepulchre in the City and a prebendary of St Paul's, was arrested for delivering an anti-Catholic sermon at Paul's Cross in 1553. He was imprisoned for eighteen months before being condemned to be burned as a heretic. His wife and eleven children met him as the sheriffs escorted him to Smithfield but, as we read in Foxe's *Book of Martyrs*, 'This sorrowful sight of his own flesh and blood could nothing move him, but that he cheerfully took his death in defence of Christ's gospel.'

The present-day West Smithfield Open Space is another of the public gardens maintained by the City Corporation. It is part of the original Smithfield (a corruption of 'smooth field'), the ancient site of tournaments, markets and executions. Bartholomew Fair was held here from the twelfth century until 1855.

The ground was laid out as a public garden in 1872. The statue in the middle was sculpted by John Birnie Philip and is entitled 'Peace'.

Moving around the corner to the north side of the cathedral we see the Paul's Cross Memorial. The column is topped by the figure of St Paul which was sculpted by the Australian artist, Sir Bertram Mackennal. The base, in the form of a pulpit, was designed by Sir Reginald Blomfield and the whole structure was erected in 1910.

Bartholomew Fair, complete with swings and roundabouts, depicted by Thomas Rowlandson.

The cost of erecting the Paul's Cross Memorial was met by Henry Charles Richards, a lawyer and an MP who had strong connections with the City of London, being a member of the Bakers' Company and of the Turners' Company. In 1880 Richards formed the City Church and Churchyard Preservation Society. He was also a member of the St Paul's Ecclesiological Society.

Next we come to the north transept and the NORTH PORTICO. The rooftop statues seen here are the original ones by Francis Bird. These five represent, from left to right, the apostles Barnabus, Philip, James the Less and Jude, and finally John the Baptist.

The pediment carving of the royal arms on a shield supported by angels and flanked by a lion and a unicorn is by Caius Gabriel Cibber.

The Monument, a 61-metre (202-foot) high fluted column of Portland stone, was designed by Wren and the City Surveyor, Robert Hooke. It was erected 1671–7 to commemorate the Great Fire of 1666. The base panel was carved by Caius Gabriel Cibber and depicts King Charles II and his brother, the Duke of York, succouring and defending the City. Cibber's second wife brought him a substantial dowry, yet he was regularly in debt. He was in prison for debt in the King's Bench at the time of carving these bas-reliefs on the Monument, but was allowed out to work during the day.

The base panel of the Monument carved by C. G. Cibber.

Dean Matthews, writing in *A History of St Paul's Cathedral* about the year he succeeded Dean Inge, said:

Financial stringency had produced by 1934 some unfortunate effects. The Dean and Chapter had let the beautiful Chapter House, one of Wren's finest works of its kind, to Lloyds Bank, which in turn had sublet part of the building . . . to the City Livery Club.

The following extracts from the Lloyds Bank Premises Committee Minute Books give some details of the transaction:

1st October, 1920

Chapter House, St Paul's, E.C.4

A proposal to rent the Chapter House for the purpose of a Branch was mentioned, and the general idea was approved if it is found that the house referred to is suitable for the purpose of our business.

21st October, 1920

Chapter House, St Paul's, E.C.4

A lease has been arranged for 21 years with option for a further 21 years at £5,000 per annum reserving one room for the Registrar.

A cheerful meeting in the Chapter House: Dean Alan Webster in the centre with, from right to left, Canon Peter Ball, Bishop Kenneth Woollcombe, Archdeacon Frank Harvey and Canon Graham Routledge.

Leaving the enclosed area by the gate at the west end of the gardens, on the right stands the CHAPTER HOUSE, a redbrick building with stone dressings. Wren's original Chapter House, built in 1711–14, was destroyed in an air-raid on 29 December 1940 and this postwar replacement was not constructed until the late 1950s. The architect was Godfrey Allen.

Regular, formal chapter meetings – that is, meetings of the Dean and the four Residentiary Canons who form the governing body of the cathedral – are held here in the first-floor Chapter Room.

The offices of the chief administrator, the Registrar and Receiver, and his staff are in the Chapter House, as are those of the St Paul's Cathedral Trust and the Secretary of the Friends of St Paul's Cathedral.

The apostle Andrew looking like Samson Agonistes.

Opposite the Chapter House there is an opportunity to see part of one of Francis Bird's rooftop statues at close quarters. Behind the railings around the north-west area of the cathedral sits the bust of the figure of St Andrew which occupied the apex position on the south transept roof until 1923. After being sent to laboratories to be tested for atmospheric pollution of the stone, it was returned to the cathedral.

Continuing westward we pass the steps to Paternoster Square before turning right into Ave Maria Lane. Some 45 metres (50 yards) down, on the opposite side of the road, is AMEN COURT. If we cross over to the corner of the court we may see, without invading the privacy of the residents, the row of three historic houses which was completed in 1673. At that time the Dean of St Paul's was also one of the four canons so the Deanery and these three houses accommodated the whole Chapter.

The first occupants of Amen Corner (as it was then known) were the canons Edward Stillingfleet who became Dean of St Paul's in 1677 and later Bishop of Worcester; Francis Turner who became Bishop of Rochester and then of Ely; and Edward Layfield who held a number of other livings concurrently.

Numbers 1, 2 and 3 Amen Court which, with the Old Deanery, housed the Chapter of St Paul's in the late seventeenth century.

There were still only three houses here until late in the nineteenth century. The most famous of all the residents was probably the writer and wit, Sydney Smith, who was appointed canon in 1831 and who moved into 1 Amen Corner in the same year. In 1839, however, he bought a house in Green Street, Grosvenor Square, and then allowed Richard Harris Barham, a minor canon and Librarian of St Paul's, to occupy the Amen Corner house. Barham, who was educated at St Paul's School and Oxford, is remembered not as a churchman but as the author of the *Ingoldsby Legends*. These humorous tales, mostly in verse, were first published in *Bentley's Miscellany* under the pseudonym Thomas Ingoldsby. His novel *My Cousin Nicholas* appeared in serial form in *Blackwood's Magazine*.

A public hanging outside Newgate prison in 1806 drawn by Rowlandson.

Barham commented that from the rear windows of the house there was 'an extensive prospect of the back of the Oxford Arms and a fine Hanging Wood in the distance'. The expression 'Hanging Wood' was a euphemism for the gallows outside Newgate Prison. In December 1870 the Dean and Chapter bought the lease of the Oxford Arms and, after the old inn was demolished they had six more houses built on the site, primarily for the minor canons. The last of those houses – 9 Amen Court – is now the Deanery.

In 1783 the practice of carting prisoners sentenced to death from Newgate to Tyburn (Marble Arch) ceased and public hangings took place at Newgate prison itself. The gallows was placed outside the door in the street called Old Bailey opposite the Magpie and Stump public house. Long before eight o'clock in the morning – the time of execution – the whole area around the prison would be packed with a mass of onlookers, including children of all ages.

It was then possible to reach Newgate prison from Amen Corner and the adjoining land. On public hanging days the sheriffs would ask permission from the Dean and Chapter to go the private way in order to avoid the unruly, and sometimes hostile, crowds.

In 1868 Virger Green wrote in his diary: 'April 27th Michael Barrett, the Fenian, was sentenced to death for the Clerkenwell explosion.' Then, a few days before a Bill to abolish public hangings became law, he wrote:

The execution of Barrett on Tuesday May 26th when a great crowd assembled. The officials, Sheriffs, etc., entered the prison by way of Amen Corner; this was the last public execution, a great relief to most people living in the neighbourhood.

We now turn back to Ludgate Hill and cross it to Dean's Court where, a little way down on the right-hand side, stands the OLD DEANERY. This has been the site of the Deanery of St Paul's since medieval times. The present building, which was constructed in 1672, cost £3000 and was paid for by the then Dean, William Sancroft, who became Archbishop of Canterbury in 1677.

The last person to live here in style with a large staff was William Ralph Inge who was Dean from 1911 to 1934. In his published diary he frequently refers to dinner parties of fourteen and his guest lists were heavily biased towards the rich and powerful. In the introduction to the diary Inge said of his period in office: 'The Dean of St Paul's was then a considerable person, to be treated with great respect and set in the seats of the mighty.'

Dean Martin Sullivan, a New Zealander, retired in 1977 and the Deanery was then, according to a surveyor's report, deemed to be unsafe until a considerable programme of renovation had been carried out. The sum of money involved was too great to be met from cathedral funds, so it was decided to lease the building to an organization that was capable of restoring it.

In 1981 the London company, Haslemere Estates, which specializes in the restoration of listed historical buildings, undertook to restore the Old Deanery. That work, and the construction of a two-storey extension at the rear, was carried out with R. Newman Ltd as the main contractors.

In January 1983 the Lord Mayor, Sir Anthony Jolliffe, attended a reception in the Old Deanery to mark the completion of the restoration; and on the last day of that month the present occupiers, a consortium of Scandinavian banks called FennoScandia, moved in. The freehold of the building is still held by the Dean and Chapter of St Paul's.

The Old Deanery in the nineteenth century: watercolour by John Crowther (left).

The restored Old Deanery (right): the rear garden and the two-storey extension designed in the style of the original building.

The next building is the OLD CHOIR SCHOOL, the front of which is in Carter Lane. The cornerstone of this building was laid on Monday, 26 January 1874. Present at that ceremony was Miss Maria Hackett, a lady who had worked and fought to improve the lives of English cathedral choristers, particularly those of St Paul's. She died on 5 November 1874, just before her 91st birthday. A few weeks later, in January 1875, the choristers moved into the building.

Almost 100 years later the Choir School moved into its present premises in New Change.

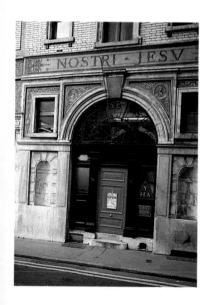

The Old Choir School, now a youth hostel.

The Old Choir School building was at the centre of the most serious disagreement between the cathedral authorities and the City Corporation since the 'Dangerous Structure' controversy in 1924. Commenting bitterly on the *Report to the Common Council of the City of London on the Precincts of St Paul's* (1956), Dean Matthews said that the planners thought of the City not as a place to live in but as a channel for the flow of motor vehicles and, to this end, they had determined that Carter Lane should be widened.

In his book *Memories and Meanings* Matthews wrote:

On one side of the Lane stood the atrociously ugly building of the telephone exchange Faraday House, and on the other our modest school. Of course, it was decided to preserve the building which ought never to have been built at all and destroy the house which had been carefully designed for its position and function. The school, almost miraculously, had survived the war and we had assumed that what our enemies had not succeeded in damaging would not be destroyed by our friends.

After all the acrimony, agreement was reached between the City and St Paul's over the site for a new Choir School and no cathedral objections were raised at the public enquiry into the plan. Ironically, the intention to demolish the north side of Carter Lane was not carried out and the Old Choir School still stands. Today it is used as a youth hostel.

The Latin wording around the frieze of the building reads MIHI AUTEM ABSIT GLORIARI NISI IN CRUCE DOMINI NOSTRI JESU CHRISTI PER QUEM MIHI MUNDUS CRUCIFIXUS EST ET EGO MUNDO. This is from Paul's Epistle to the Galatians, and in the *Bible in Basic English* it reads: 'But far be it from me to have glory in anything, but only in the cross of our Lord Jesus Christ, through which this world has come to an end on the cross for me, and I for it.'

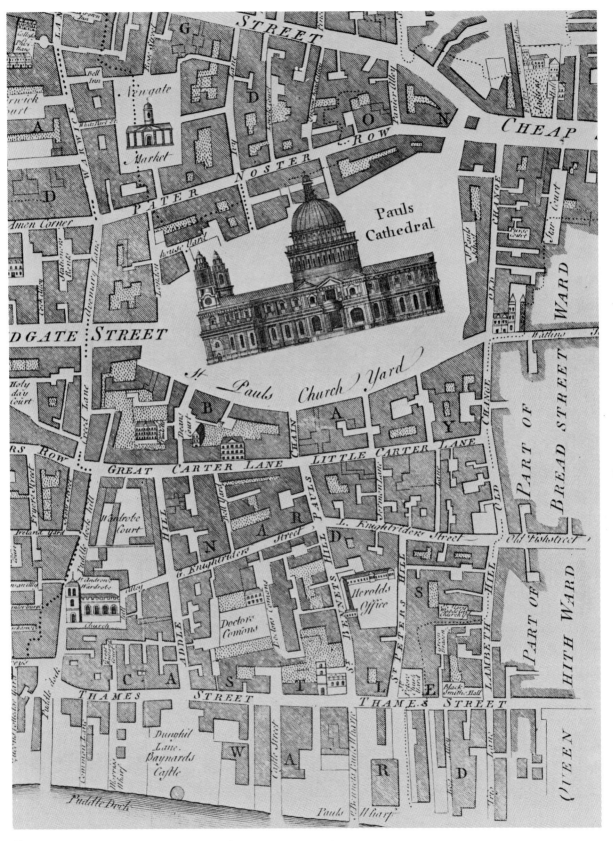

Willsm
Phi:
sians

NEWgate
LANE

Bell
Inn

G   STREET

Newgate
Market

White.Ret St

D

LANCASTER

Alley

CHEAP

N

Paternoster Alley

Pauls
Cathedral

St Pauls
Mddret

CHANGE

New Court

Panse
Court

PATER   NOSTER   ROW

Queen
Inn

Brwick
Court

A

D

Warwick Lane

Amen Corner

Katherine
Rents

Stinemary Lane

London

ouse Yard

London House Yard

Holly
day
Court

DGATE   STREET

Deans
Court

B

St   Pauls   Church   Yard

A

Y

CHAIN

Watling

PART   OF
BREAD   STREET   WARD

RS   ROW

Fryers
Alley

Freed Lane

GREAT   CARTER   LANE

LITTLE   CARTER   LANE

CREED

SERMANLANE

OLD   CHANGE

PAULS

Ireland yard

Wardrobe
Court

Puddle docks Hill

HILL

N

A

R

D.

L.   Knightriders   Street

St Anto:e's
Wardrobe

Church

ST   BENNET'S   HILL

G.   Knightriders   Street

Doctors   Comons

Herolds
Office

S

Maq Maqdalen
Church

Part of

QUEEN

Paul's Back Comons

PADDLE

ST   PETER'S   HILL

HITH   WARD

HILL

C   A   S   T   L   E

E

Black
Smith: Hall

Thames s: Quay

THAMES   STREET

Morris Wharf

Puddle dock

Cameron Lane

THAMES   STREET

W   A   R   D

Dunghil
Lane
Baynards
Castle

Castle   Street

Trigg Lane

Isle Lane

Paddle Dock

St Benets Pauls Wharf

Pauls   Wharf

Old Fishstreet

We now return eastwards along Carter Lane towards the cathedral. After some 45 metres (50 yards) Godliman Street crosses the lane. If we stop here and look right, towards the river, we shall see the Wren church of St Benet's, Paul's Wharf. The site of the church is just to the north of where, in Christopher Wren's day, there were two landing stages – Baynards Castle Wharf and Paul's Wharf.

Stone for the building of the new cathedral was shipped from the Isle of Portland off the Dorset coast to the Pool of London. There it was transferred to barges which discharged their cargoes at one or other of those two wharfs.

Opposite St Benet's is the College of Arms, founded in 1484. State occasions at St Paul's are attended by the Officers of Arms.

The church of St Benet's, Paul's Wharf, completed in 1685, was built by Thomas Strong, Wren's master mason on the building of St Paul's. It is constructed of brick with stone quoins and stone garlands over the windows.

Since 1879 St Benet's has been the Metropolitan Church for Welsh Episcopalians.

The Lord Mayor, Sir Alan Traill, stopping at the south portico to be greeted by the Dean and Chapter, November 1984.

It may surprise us today to learn that the sailors involved in this domestic coastal shipping of stone at the turn of the seventeenth century faced other hazards in addition to the vagaries of the weather. The Building Accounts of St Paul's for October 1706 (as transcribed in *The Wren Society* Vol. XV) include an entry which reads: 'To Henry Perry for Portland Stone and Freight.'

This is followed by:

Memo. The sd Perry was taken by a French Privateer in Oct 1705 and carried to Calais, where his Vessell was condemned as Prize. Some time after Perry came for England among exchanged Prisoners, and the Ship & Loading were sold to one Sam Green, a merchant in Rotterdam, wch Perry hearing of went for Holland and bought the sd Ship & Loading of the sd Green, and brought the same to London, where the sd stone was bought of him for St Pauls at ye usual prices, he first producing the condemnation of the sd Ship at Calais, the Bill of Sale there to Green, & Green's Bill of Sale to him. The Ship is called the *Phoenix of London*.

Continuing further along Carter Lane we come to a public garden on the left with a broad path running through it. From this path the whole of the SOUTH FACE of the cathedral may be surveyed. Directly opposite is the south transept surmounted by its five apostles and, behind them, the marvellous dome riding high.

Our last look should be at the pediment carving by Cibber, to remind ourselves that there has been a Christian church on this site since AD 604. Perhaps St Paul's, like Perry's ship, might also be called The Phoenix of London.

Index

Figures in **bold** type refer to the City text; figures in *italic* refer to illustrations